The Reluctant Republican

UNIVERSITY PRESS OF FLORIDA

Florida A&M University, Tallahassee
Florida Atlantic University, Boca Raton
Florida Gulf Coast University, Ft. Myers
Florida International University, Miami
Florida State University, Tallahassee
New College of Florida, Sarasota
University of Central Florida, Orlando
University of Florida, Gainesville
University of North Florida, Jacksonville
University of South Florida, Tampa
University of West Florida, Pensacola

The Constitution of the United States

Preamble

We The People of the United States, in order to form a more perfect union, establish justice, ensure domestic tranquility, provide for the common defence, promote the general welfare, and secure the blessings of liberty to ourselves and our posterity, do ordain and establish this Constitution for the United States of America.

Ratified June 21, 1788

The Reluctant Republican

My Fight for

the Moderate Majority

Barbara F. Olschner

University Press of Florida

Gainesville / Tallahassee / Tampa / Boca Raton

Pensacola / Orlando / Miami / Jacksonville / Ft. Myers / Sarasota

VIVA FLORIDA 500
1513–2013

A Florida Quincentennial Book

Printed in the United States of America. This book is printed on Glatfelter Natures Book,
a paper certified under the standards of the Forestry Stewardship Council (FSC). It is a
recycled stock that contains 30 percent postconsumer waste and is acid-free.

This book may be available in an electronic edition.

18 17 16 15 14 13   6 5 4 3 2 1

Library of Congress Cataloging-in-Publication Data
Olschner, Barbara F.
The reluctant Republican : my fight for the moderate majority / Barbara F. Olschner.
p. cm.
ISBN 978-0-8130-4453-8 (alk. paper)
1. Olschner, Barbara F. 2. Political campaigns—Florida. 3. Florida. Legislature. Senate—
Elections. 4. Florida—Politics and government. I. Title.
F316.23.O43A3 2013
975.9'064092—dc23   2012039458

The University Press of Florida is the scholarly publishing agency for the State University
System of Florida, comprising Florida A&M University, Florida Atlantic University,
Florida Gulf Coast University, Florida International University, Florida State University,
New College of Florida, University of Central Florida, University of Florida, University
of North Florida, University of South Florida, and University of West Florida.

University Press of Florida
15 Northwest 15th Street
Gainesville, FL 32611-2079
http://www.upf.com

To two strong and independent southern women
to whom I owe my character and my heart:
my mother, Evelyn Lilley Olschner,
and my aunt, Thelma "Sister" Lilley Blackmore

Contents

Preface

Being a conservative in America traditionally has meant
that one holds a deep, abiding respect for the Constitution.

Barry Goldwater, September 1981

I have long thought of myself as a "traditional" conservative in the
sense that Senator Goldwater had in mind when he wrote these
words more than thirty years ago—a time that in hindsight seems
so long ago. I was a freshman in law school when Senator Goldwater
said he saw "the Religious Right as a threat to the Constitution and
to American values." A conservative like Senator Goldwater could
not pass the litmus test of today's GOP. Goldwater was pro-choice,
considered himself an "honorary homosexual" for supporting gay
rights, and once famously suggested "Christians should line up and
kick Jerry Falwell's ass." Hardly a platform for today's "true conservative."

By the time I ran for Congress on the Republican ticket in 2010,
the Constitution had been pushed so far to the margin of American
politics that many extreme right-wing candidates would win over
qualified and experienced moderates. The controlling culture of the
Republican Party demanded, above all else, a strict allegiance to
party ideology. This was the wave that the Tea Party helped to create,
and the Republican Party was riding it to success in 2010 in Florida,
as well as nationally. In this climate, like others who would suffer

similar defeats as a result of the wave of right-wing rage and resentment, I was clearly a misfit. I was a political novice, and it could be said that I was just unprepared and underfunded for a congressional race, but that wouldn't be the whole truth. No one was prepared to combat this bloodthirsty cry for ideological purity. Politicians far more experienced and successful than I were crushed by this right-wing tsunami.

The senior senator from Alaska, Lisa Murkowski, lost her primary in 2010 to Joe Miller, a Tea Party–movement candidate also supported by Sarah Palin. Senator Murkowski, a moderate Republican, mounted a write-in campaign in the general election and was able to retain her seat, despite having to file a lawsuit when Miller would not concede defeat. She remains one of the few moderate Republicans in the U.S. Senate with John McCain, Susan Collins, Tom Cochran, Lamar Alexander, and Charles Grassley.

Mike Castle served his state of Delaware as governor and congressman for four decades as a centrist Republican. Because of his experience and name recognition, he was expected to defeat the Democrat in the contest for Vice President Joe Biden's Senate seat. However, he lost in the primary to the Palin-endorsed Tea Party favorite Christine O'Donnell. As the only public figure since the 1600s to feel the need to publicly proclaim that she was "not a witch," O'Donnell became an easy target for the parodists on *Saturday Night Live*. She would suffer a resounding loss against Democrat Chris Coons in the general election, but she "felt good" about the outcome, hailing it as a victory for the Tea Party, notwithstanding the Republicans' loss of a Senate seat.

It is easy to call these races bizarre, but they typified the prevailing mood in 2010 when I threw my hat into the ring. I was connected to neither the Republican establishment nor the right-wing conservative ideology. Although I believed in the basic principles of the GOP, I was moderate and pragmatic. I did not then, and do not now, think that a party dominated by a single, narrowly defined ideology or agenda is good for America. I thought, and still think, that America needs an open and serious debate of the issues critically important to the nation—not just endless, sometimes mindless, repetition of the same old mantras that pass for political thought nowadays. I had no idea that advocating such moderation would be a recipe for disaster in a congressional race in 2010, and in political contests throughout 2012.

Considering the challenges facing our nation when I entered this race, I thought that a moderate approach was reasonable, rather than some sort of heresy against the true Republican path. During the campaign, however, an older woman once yelled out to me in a harsh tone: "Standing in the middle of the road is a good way to get hit by cars going both ways." I must confess that her statement shocked me into silence. I was experiencing firsthand something I had not expected when I entered the political arena: the vitriol the right wing directed at the moderates in their own party.

I wished I had remembered at that moment what President Eisenhower said: "People talk about the middle of the road as though it were unacceptable. Actually, all human problems, excepting morals, come into the gray areas. Things are not all black and white. There have to be compromises. The middle of the road is all of the usable surface. The extremes, right and left, are in the gutters."

Although I admit to being a political neophyte, when I entered my congressional race I was a courtroom lawyer with twenty-five years of arguing cases in front of a jury. I was well versed in discussing complex factual issues and legal principles with ordinary men and women of the jury as I tried more than a hundred cases to verdict, most with outstanding results. It was my experience that people from all backgrounds could understand the most complicated facts and legal principles, and over 90 percent of the time, would reach the correct verdict. I thought these same men and women would approach the serious issues facing our country in a similar manner. I was dead wrong.

I thought that the average voter, like the average juror, would respond to reason and logic. But I learned that reason and logic sometimes fail because political problems often evoke responses more visceral than rational. At this time in our country's history, only compromise, civility, and intelligence will solve our problems. But the nation's focus is on the extreme agendas of each party, fueled by partisan pundits, biased media outlets, and self-serving political parties.

I knew, of course, that the "fringe element" in politics provides irresistible fodder for the media. I had just always assumed that fringe individuals had no real control over the outcome of an election, rarely ran for office, and, quite frankly, were not in my backyard. I was also well acquainted with the numerous polls that indicated that less than 26 percent of all voters consider themselves either liberal or conservative and that 65 percent consider themselves moderate. So I assumed that, as a moderate, I would be talking to the majority of voters. I would find myself wrong on that assumption as well.

I wrote this book for the same reason I ran for Congress: I wanted to speak truthfully about the issues in this country in order to solve them. I was politically naïve and finished in last place, but this is not a story about losing—it is about what passes for politics in this country and the leaders we elect. I played the political game poorly. The rules of engagement do not reward those who speak truthfully; current politics is about pandering for votes and money. I could have walked away when I didn't raise enough money. I could have withdrawn when I realized I did not meet the current definition of a true conservative. I could have just gone back to the practice of law and said, "Politics is not for me." There was no real need to write this book, but there was one reason.

For the first fifty-eight years of my life, I do not consider that I ever made any significant contribution to my country, other than the ones most of us make as we work, raise our families, pay taxes, and occasionally support a candidate we know or like. In 2010, my patriotic conscience was pricked, and I decided to offer my time and talents as a citizen legislator, not a professional politician. But what I saw—not only in my race, but nationally as well—convinced me this was not just a regional story about the Florida Panhandle, and that compelled me to share this story.

The 2010 midterm election did, of course, return the House of Representatives to the Republicans, but there is nothing particularly new about such a sudden shift—it has happened many times. What was new was the uncompromising zealotry of many of the newly elected Republicans, and this view from inside the tent illustrates not only the foolishness of this trend, but also how dangerous it is for the future of the Republican Party and this great country.

As with all great experiences, I gained a new understanding through the campaign process that I found valuable. I began with a perception of an overreaching liberal agenda that had little regard for the constraints of the Constitution. I ended with a deep concern over the imposition of a right-wing agenda with little regard for constitutional authority. But, in light of the way events have unfolded since 2010, with the political demise of moderate Republicans like Senator Olympia Snowe and Senator Dick Lugar, I believe both the problem and the solution lie with the moderates and the centrists of both parties. When we lose capable elected officials who can dialogue thoughtfully with those of differing views, we lose not only the voice of reason, but also the majority of Americans.

This brief and painful foray into politics taught me what I believe is an important lesson for U.S. citizens, our parties, and the nation. Those who bring a strict and unyielding ideology to politics, those who want only "their America," those who are resistant to compromise or intolerant of the views of others, will not welcome this message. This book is written for the majority of Americans who consider themselves moderates—centrists and those more interested in the success of America than the success of any political party. Those of us who occupy the "usable part of the road" must be willing to come forward and speak with the strong voice of compromise to lead this country forward. As you read this book, I think the reason for that message will become crystal clear.

1

The Competition

Article I. Section 1.

All legislative Powers herein granted shall be vested
in a Congress of the United States, which shall consist
of a Senate and House of Representatives.

I went incognito to my first public candidate forum. I hadn't intended
to begin my campaign in disguise, but nevertheless, on January
20, 2010, prior to submitting my official paperwork to become a
candidate for Congress in Florida's District 2, I went to a congressional candidates' forum in Walton County, the southern portion of
which lies within District 2, where I live.

I was, to be honest, a political novice. Until that time, my political
involvement had been confined to local politics: campaigning to elect
the first woman to the Walton County Commission, fund-raising, attending candidate forums and bake sales. Not only does local politics
offer an opportunity to meet potential voters, but attendance at the
right events also suggests shared values. The northwest portion of
the Panhandle is said to resemble Alabama more than Florida in culture and attitude, and is sometimes referred to as "L.A.," or "Lower
Alabama." One of the shared cultural values is the importance of
guns, which is evidenced in residents' attachment to vehicles that
can incorporate a gun rack. This was duly noted in the presidential
primary by Newt Gingrich, who demeaned the Chevy Volt because
"You can't put a gun rack in a Volt."

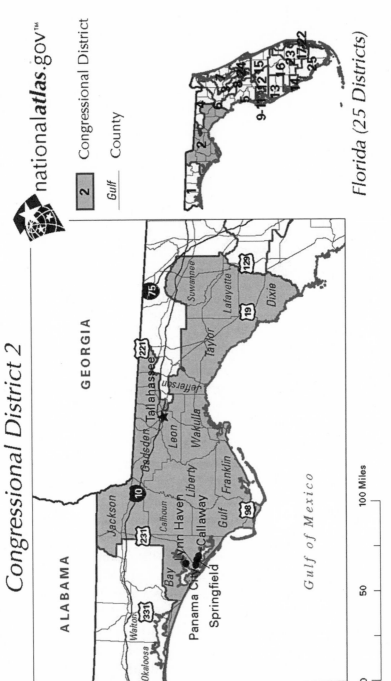

Congressional District 2

nationalatlas.gov™

| 2 | Congressional District |

Gulf — County

Florida (25 Districts)

Map of Florida Congressional District 2 in 2010. The district was composed of sixteen counties and two main population areas: Panama City and Tallahassee.

While campaigning for others, I learned the importance of courting this vote, which required attendance at local gun shops and gun events, especially, the annual NRA-sponsored banquet. At my first NRA banquet, I was surprised to see young women—all barefoot and some pregnant—walking between the tables showcasing the various rifles and weaponry. These were clearly local women, not models from runways or car shows, either members themselves or recruited by a relative NRA member. In thirty years of living in Birmingham, Alabama, I had attended a lot of civic banquets, but never one quite like this. I knew "barefoot and pregnant" as a figure of speech, but I had never witnessed it in a public setting. While these girls paraded up and down the aisles between long tables, I mentioned to my table-mates that this was "my first redneck rifle catwalk." Although they found the phrase humorous, they were quick to point out that I was the one out of my element. As one local woman said to me, "Women with rifles—that's nothing special in the Panhandle."

So, on a briskly cold January night in 2010, I walked into the South Walton County Library Annex, where I had been many times for various county meetings. The meeting room is starkly lit, with vanilla walls, padded folding chairs, a lectern, and the U.S. flag propped in a corner waiting for allegiance to be sworn. It looks like a room where you might endure hours of boredom punctuated by minutes of emotional drama and the unbridled tirades of concerned citizens.

Many faces in that room were familiar: current and former county officials, candidates for upcoming elections, the local Republican posse, and a few well-known citizen agitators. But there were a number of folks who seemed to have just wandered in the door—an older, seasoned crowd. Although the meeting began at 6:00 p.m., this was not an after-work crowd; it was more a time-on-our-hands crowd. This was the beach, after all. The dress was decidedly casual, as if people had spotted an unusual number of cars in the library parking lot on their way to Home Depot and decided to turn in and investigate.

The South Walton County Republican Club had sponsored the meeting, and although I knew many of the people there, I had not yet informed anyone of my decision to run. In hindsight, all of this seems a little odd, even to me. I had gotten into the race late, even for an August primary. There was an incredible amount to do and not enough money to hire all the essential help—I had only a few well-connected friends operating as my campaign staff.

It is easy now to see all the mistakes I made in running this congressional campaign. I brought certain character traits to this endeavor that, unfortunately, were not very helpful in the political process. I was not nearly narcissistic enough to be in politics. The notion of "Me, Me, Me" interjected into every conversation did not appeal to me. Viewing every political event as another photo op seemed superficial to me, and when I was instructed to post such photos on Facebook, I did so reluctantly. That night in the library annex, however, I was employing certain traits that had served me well both on the tennis court and in the courtroom—I was checking out my opponents.

I started playing tennis when I was eight years old with my father, who was an accomplished player. After graduating from the University of North Carolina at Charlotte, I made a sparse-but-fun living teaching and playing tennis. For seven years, I was the head professional—and the only professional—at Bogue Banks Country Club in Pine Knoll Shores, North Carolina, where I grew up. For six months I would teach tennis, and for the rest of the year I would head to North Miami Beach to train and play on the Avon Futures Circuit, the satellite circuit for the now-defunct Virginia Slims Tour. Playing on the circuit over the years, I had come to know many of the players, but there were new ones every year—former high-ranking juniors who had been out of tennis because of marriage, injury, or emotional meltdowns. The foreign girls—especially those from economically depressed communist countries like Romania and the Soviet Union—were the most difficult to read. They were not averse to cheating and generally spoke little English. When it came to the score, they only remembered it when it was in their favor, and their limited English made further discussion difficult. A close match against a foreign player with marginal English and a hulking serious boyfriend or girlfriend peering in through the fence usually ended in defeat.

When I did not know my next opponent, I would watch her play from the sidelines where I wouldn't be noticed and recognized as I

From 1975 to 1980, I was a professional tennis player. I played on the Avon Futures Circuit and taught tennis as a member of USPTA, and was also the head women's tennis coach at East Carolina University. I still love coaching tournament players and, when I am injury-free, playing in senior national tournaments.

tried to determine strengths and weaknesses. I would also decide whether it was a match I could win outright, meaning strength against strength, or whether I needed to devise another strategy. My "A game" was serve-and-volley—moving to the net as soon as possible after the serve to hit a winning shot out of the air instead of off the bounce. When you serve and volley, you take chances to shorten the points, and the longer you play, generally the more errors you make. Most girls played a baseline game—staying in the back of the court, looking for the right angle and distance. I could not hang back and hit with these girls from the baseline because my ground strokes were not that consistent or accurate. But, more, I liked the risk and the action; I tended to get bored hitting the same repetitive shots until someone cracked under the pressure.

My "B game" was cat-and-mouse, employing backspin, sidespin, slices, drop shots, and lobs. It wasn't a game I was proud of, but it was effective. I'd learned it from my father—my default game when I was losing or tired. The "B game" was annoying old-school tactics, and not a game that won you any admiration. So I would watch my next opponent and try to determine whether I could play my real game or whether I had to play like a hack to win.

My father, Joseph C. Olschner, also introduced me to the courtroom game—I had grown up watching him try cases, and as a southern country lawyer he taught me not only about the courtroom but also how to read and make judgments based on numerous factors, about jurors, judges, witnesses, or other lawyers. By the time I began the practice of law in 1984 in Birmingham, Alabama, my father had died of a heart attack in the courtroom. But the lessons he taught me over the years remained with me, such as the advice to check out your opponents.

I would often observe certain other lawyers to see how they played the game. I would walk in quietly, sit in the back of the courtroom, and observe the interaction between that particular lawyer and the judge, the witnesses, the opposing lawyers, and the jury. Having seen enough to determine the caliber of the lawyer—which could take seconds or minutes—I would leave as quietly as I came in, only later stopping by to visit judges in chambers to tell them what I'd observed. Being restricted to the role of umpires rather than players, the judges were always curious and loved discussing the strategy of the courtroom game. Or, maybe it was, as my father had said, because "lawyers love to gossip."

So I was used to being a competitor who carefully checks out the competition before the game. And this seemed liked a good approach to the game of politics, given my inexperience. Withdrawing from the race was still an option if the competition seemed too fierce. Three candidates showed up, not including the one lurking in the room: Eddie Hendry, Charles Ranson, and Steve Southerland.

Hendry looked like he had been in the car for hours, and as he lived in Tallahassee (more than 150 miles away) and sold pharmaceuticals for a living, he had probably logged hundreds of miles that day alone. In 2008, Eddie had run for this same seat, losing in the primary to Mark Mulligan with only 32 percent of the vote. The early campaign signs proclaiming "Hendry for Congress" were already on display in Bay, Walton, and Leon Counties, presumably promotional material left over from his last race.

Eddie, a graduate of the Citadel and former Army captain, had a bulldog feistiness to his personality and physical appearance. He comes from Taylor County, a very rural eastern part of the district where it is not unusual to see Confederate flags unfurled on small front porches. Some of that Confederate fight is in Eddie as well. Maybe the miles logged that day had tired him, or maybe he knew better than the rest how arduous this campaign process was, but that night, he seemed uncomfortable. He pulled his head back away from people and did not approach voters to meet and talk with them. He kept his arms folded in front of him in a protective stance over a wrinkled navy suit. He did not take advantage of the opportunity to meet and attract voters or supporters, and seemed weary at the beginning of the race.

The other two candidates were socially comfortable, though in completely different ways. Charlie Ranson is a lawyer from Tallahassee, a former assistant attorney general of Florida, sixty-three years old, tall, distinguished, well dressed, and seeming very much like a congressional candidate—smart, articulate, and well spoken.

He was, however, not an extrovert, and while he was at ease speaking to people, he was a little out of his element with this group

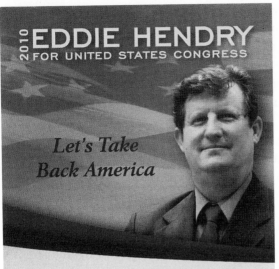

2010 EDDIE HENDRY
FOR UNITED STATES CONGRESS

Let's Take Back America

"I am running for Congress because I care about our future - for both my family and yours.

"I care about protecting our rights - and keeping government out of our doctors' offices.

"I care about the legacy we leave our children and grandchildren - and stopping Washington from adding trillions more in insurmountable debt to their shoulders.

"I care about creating the jobs our families need - and a fair tax code that ensures they keep what they earn.

"Together, I believe we can take back our country - and get real results for North Florida."

Eddie Hendry

- Sixth generation North Floridian
- Married to Angela for 22 years
- Two teenagers, Courtney and Grant
- Former U.S. Army officer and graduate of the Citadel
- Successful businessman
- Proud member of the NRA, American Heart Association, and American Diabetes Association

www.EddieHendryForCongress.com

Flier for candidate Eddie Hendry. The first of the Tea Party–inspired "Take Back America" slogans, with emphasis on his family, longevity as a Floridian, military service, and ever-important NRA membership.

from Walton County—an intelligent and sophisticated lawyer from Tallahassee talking with beach folks wearing Crocs and Topsiders who had abandoned their former lives and landed in the Florida Panhandle.

Even though he bent stiffly at the waist as he shook my hand, I liked his courtly manner as he asked if we had met before. We were, after all, lawyers from the same part of the state. "No," I told him, "I don't think we have." But I was thinking, "We will be seeing a lot of each other in the future, however." He nodded, as if not knowing what to say next, smiled politely, and moved on. My first impression was that small talk was not his forte.

In his closing remarks that night, Ranson said that his family was fine if he failed at this endeavor. That seemed a strange remark to make at the beginning of the race, and I wondered then if he was committed for the long run of a campaign. By the end of the evening, though, it was clear that Charlie Ranson was the most intelligent and articulate of the three candidates.

The third candidate was used to working crowds he didn't know. Steve Southerland, the undertaker from Panama City, had positioned himself by the front door. He leaned forward at the waist with a deep, obsequious bow. His extended right hand was meaty and clammy. His smile was not warm—more like the pattern of a smile. He narrowed his eyes in a kind of squint and opened his mouth showing his teeth. His manner toward everyone never varied, no matter their age or gender, as if the funeral business had taught him to greet all strangers with feigned sympathy.

Although he was almost fifteen years my junior, he seemed much older. I could see that greeting strangers was his bread and butter and would be an advantage for him. But I was completely unprepared when he began to speak.

"Have you had enough?" He was using the wireless microphone—unnecessary in a room that small—and his words echoed off the walls. "I've had enough," he said. "My family, all twenty-three members, has had enough! We have *had* enough."

Wow, I thought to myself. *That's a big family. Was he Mormon?*

"I've had enough!" He began to raise his voice. "My wife has had enough!" He tugged at his belt. "My four daughters have had enough."

Fighting for Gulf Coast Values

STEVE SOUTHERLAND
FOR CONGRESS

www.southerlandforcongress.com

850-866-2440

Flier for candidate Steve Southerland. Southerland's first flier was all about fighting for values and new leadership in Washington. He was a leader, he said, because he was "first out of the birth canal."

OK, so the immediate family is only six folks. But are his daughters old enough to have a political view of national issues? And how does that come up in a family discussion with children? I had this vision of everyone sitting around the dinner table beating on the table with forks and spoons, shouting, "We've had enough! We've had enough!"

"Even my yellow Lab has had enough!" Southerland grinned, as he looked around the room, satisfied that he had established his family values.

Does anyone else find it troubling that he's claiming to know the political persuasion of his dog? Are all yellow Labs Republicans?

Southerland wandered around the front of the room looking more like he was giving his first karaoke performance at a bowling alley than like someone running for Congress. Both of the other candidates at the dais looked at him from beneath lowered eyelids as if they were afraid to look straight on at this spectacle. He seemed to be picking up steam, emboldened by his mantra of "Have you had enough?" He leaned forward toward the crowd holding the microphone with a death grip.

"Do you know what I tell my children when the president comes on television?" He turned to look at the other side of the room and shouted, "DO YOU KNOW WHAT I TELL THEM?" He stood up tall and shouted toward the back of the room: "Know what I tell them?"

Now he seemed to get really angry as he spit out the next words in a tone and manner we refer to in the South as "scary redneck": "'Look away!' I tell them. 'Look AWAY! LOOK AWAY!'"

Isn't this the guy who has raised the most money so far? I thought to myself while looking around the room.

"Any time"—and here he spit out the name—"*Obama* comes on TV." He screamed in a loud, scary, domineering voice, "LOOK AWAY!! And DO you know WHY?"

The only thing that came to mind was: *Because you are insane? Because you are a raging control freak?*

Southerland lowered his voice as if he were revealing a great secret, gestured with his index finger toward his temple, nodded his head knowingly, and said in a conspiratorial tone, "Because if you don't see him, and just listen to him speak, you don't get fooled by him, and you see what he is saying."

Southerland was saying that the only way you could get taken in by President Obama was if you looked at him. *This* was the front-runner? I couldn't believe it. But the best was yet to come. During the question-and-answer period, each candidate was asked a question from the audience and given sixty seconds to answer. One audience member asked, "What leadership abilities qualify you for this office?"

Ranson went first and spoke of his background as a lawyer and assistant attorney general, working with the legislators to resolve complex issues. He spoke of his dedication to his family and to the future of this country for his family and the families of others. He seemed to me a quiet, intelligent person who would lead with consideration and civility.

Eddie Hendry spoke of the leadership traits he learned at the Citadel and in the Army. He said he would stand and fight for what he believed in and that his strong convictions gave him the ability to lead others. It was the normal sort of thing people say when they run for office. But I was not at all prepared for the next candidate's response.

Southerland stood up and tugged at his belt. He paused for a moment as if wanting to be sure everyone was focused on him. He raised himself to his full height and said with pride: "Well," he said, "my leadership abilities are based on the fact that I was first out of the birth canal."

What? I thought. *Was he joking?* I looked around the room to see if anyone else found this statement crazy. I could not detect anyone who did, although I thought I saw Eddie raise an eyebrow.

"I am the oldest of four siblings," he continued. "Being first out of the birth canal makes me a leader. In our family business, I am the leader. When there is only five seconds left on the clock in our business, they toss the ball to me. They know I can handle it."

In the funeral business? What time is left on the clock that matters?

Strolling around the room, he seemed happy to share more about his life. "My proudest moment in life was at twenty-five years old, when my father took me into his office, and said, 'My chair is now your chair.'" Southerland's voice got a little husky as if remembering this event was emotional for him even now. He glanced at his father sitting in the front row with his cane propped across his lap. He nodded at his father as he repeated his father's words: "'Son, today you are the leader of the family business.' That was my proudest moment."

I still did not understand how being born first gave you leadership ability. Wasn't the feudal practice of male primogeniture—by which the eldest son takes everything—a vestige of monarchies, not democracies? I am a southerner, and I confess that I know a few families, mostly farming families, who still hold to such a view, but I thought they were in a distinct minority.

Eddie stood up and showed some tenacity. "As an officer at the Citadel, I know that men are trained to be leaders and that birth order and 'birth right' do not make a man a leader." He said he was surprised that Steve would make such a statement. But Southerland just sat with a smug expression on his face, nodding as if to say that the real people, whoever they were, knew what he was talking about. As I looked around the room, I did not see anyone who looked as shocked as I'd felt on hearing such a statement. Perhaps that should have spoken volumes to me; sadly, it did not.

Ranson did not move a muscle. It was clear that he was not about to go down the "birth canal" road, not even to be a congressman. I was beginning to like Mr. Ranson.

Although it had been difficult to make the decision to enter this race, seeing the competition had made me eager to participate. While Ranson clearly had the intellectual upper hand, he seemed reluctant to get into the fray. Hendry was not afraid to throw a punch, but so far, he did not seem able to land one. And while Southerland had the funeral director's gift of gab with folks, he seemed kind of nutty.

A current Walton County commissioner and friend, Sara Commander, was in the audience that night, campaigning for reelection. As things were winding down, I leaned over to her and asked her what she thought. Sara is a true local, born and bred in Walton County. She lives in the northern part of the county and would not be voting in this congressional district, but she knows the county. She nodded toward Southerland as she said, "Well, you know, my family was in the funeral business, too. And, well, he has that way of talking that folks like." I wanted to ask her whether she thought voters might be put off by his bizarre ideas, like being first out of the birth canal, but I did not. Surely, I thought to myself, if the voters hear this guy, they will never vote for him, much less contribute the kind of money needed for a congressional campaign.

I left the library that night thinking that the voters surely must understand the seriousness of the issues we faced and would want a person in Congress who was equipped to address those issues— and not just talk in a manner that folks liked. I thought Mr. Ranson would be my toughest opponent. I felt I could play my "A game" against all three.

I couldn't have been more wrong. This was a game I knew nothing about. Ranson would bow out of the race and throw his endorsement to me. Southerland would go on to win the primary and the general election.

2

The Odds

Article I. Section 2. Clause 2.

No person shall be a Representative who shall not have
attained to the age of twenty-five years, and been seven years
a citizen of the United States, and who shall not, when elected,
be an inhabitant of that state in which he shall be chosen.

That night at the library I was also able to hear the serious and
complex issues that concerned the voters—issues that concerned me as well. And I knew that my education, training,
and experience had equipped me to deal with these issues. Although
many people with political aspirations plan for years before entertaining a decision to run, mine had been reached in fewer than thirty
days.

"Allen Boyd's seat is vulnerable," a friend, neighbor, and former
local politician had said to me over dinner in early January 2010. "I
thought about running for his seat, but it is not the right time for
me. He is going to lose. You should run."

"Me? I've never been interested in politics or a political career."

"But you're smart, conservative, a lawyer, you understand the issues, and you have a background in public speaking. Voters are tired
of politicians. I'm telling you, this is a seat that can be won, and not
being a politician is a good thing. This is a chance for you to do something for your country."

That last sentence hit home.

My only prior involvement in politics had been helping other candidates get elected. Although I'm an extrovert who likes people, I've never had a feel for political nuance. As a lawyer, I was known for being straightforward, direct, and fearless, with a bit of the wit that most trial lawyers possess. That same wit did not always work on the campaign trail, as I found out when I was campaigning for a local official. We had gone to north Walton County to meet with some influential voters at the "general store," which really was just a Tom Thumb convenience store. We sat in the back of the store with a group of six white men early one Sunday morning, the men doing most of the talking. One man, dressed in a red-and-black plaid flannel shirt, said to me while sipping coffee, "So when are you going to run for office?"

"Well," I said in jest, "the only thing I've ever been interested in was the Skeeter Board." I was referring in the local vernacular to the Mosquito Control Board. I thought the term "Skeeter Board" was funny, and though I knew mosquito control was important, it seemed to me that the regulatory board should be appointed rather than elected. The man shook his head and said, "Why would you want to do that?" "Well, it is a paid position and you do get health insurance," I said repeating what I had heard other candidates say about the position.

The man stopped sipping coffee and began to shake his head vigorously from side to side and said seriously, "Oh, No. No, No, No. You do not want to do that! I'll tell you why: My cousin was on the Skeeter Board and he went up in the plane as a spotter. Well, he went up, but he didn't come down." He looked at me and nodded with a sad look. "I mean, he came down, but he didn't come down the right way—if you get my drift." He made a motion with his hand to indicate a plane in a nosedive and his fingers crashed into the tabletop. He shook his head and his voice took on a sad and sincere tone as he said, "So, I really don't think it would be a good idea for you to be on the Skeeter Board."

I realized my attempt at humor had fallen flat, so I nodded seriously and said, "I see. I didn't know that. I will certainly have to rethink this." I decided it was better to not make any further attempts at humor, and we continued to discuss local politics. Everything was fine until right before we were leaving when the man in the flannel shirt stopped everything and said: "Hold on, Hold on! Hey, I've been thinking, and I think I've got this figured out." Everyone turned to look at him with perplexed expressions. "Skeeter Board—I've figured out how she can be on Skeeter Board." Speaking earnestly, he said, "Here's what you do: When they come to you and ask you to be a spotter and go up in the plane to look for skeeters, you just say, 'No.' Problem solved," he said, pleased as punch. The other men nodded earnestly as well.

As we walked toward the car, the candidate I was helping suggested, "Don't try to be funny in politics." I realized that my sense of humor might not translate in politics, and so I resolved to be absolutely serious about running for Congress.

Allen Boyd was a Blue Dog Democrat, one of those who identified themselves as fiscal conservatives and generally were more

Allen Boyd, former congressman from Florida's District 2, served in the U.S. House of Representatives from 1996 to 2010. Boyd was one of the "flip-flop five"—representatives who changed their earlier "no" vote on ObamaCare to "yes." It probably cost him the election. This has been a white male Democrat seat for the majority of the last 130 years, but it did not start out that way.

willing to vote with Republicans on fiscal issues than their more liberal peers.

Boyd had served in the House of Representatives for fourteen years, winning his seat easily every time. During the beginning months of the Obama administration, Boyd voted 94.6 percent of the time with Nancy Pelosi, the Speaker of the Democrat-controlled House of Representatives. Boyd had voted for cap and trade legislation, the economic stimulus, and Obama's health-care plan. Whenever Boyd appeared at town hall meetings during the summer of 2009, it was obvious that the conservatives in his district were hopping mad.

One comment posted on www.redstates.com/retiretherinos/, in response to "Sarah Palin has targeted Allen Boyd" said this:

> Boyd is trash. He had an affair and his 40-year marriage ended. He voted for socialism in a district McCain got 54% of the vote in and the district is probably even more Republican in a mid-term. The Republicans need to target Boyd and believe they will. Until the healthcare vote Boyd was a very moderate Dem. He has a primary challenger from a black state senator named Al Lawson. The district is almost a quarter black and if Lawson won the primary he would lose in the general for sure.

Like many Americans, and all Republicans, I was deeply and fundamentally concerned about the direction of this country. It seemed to me that the agenda on the left was hijacking the country and holding hostage everyone who disagreed. I had carefully followed the debate on the Patient Protection and Affordable Care Act—ObamaCare, as the Republicans dubbed it. My law practice had been heavily involved in medical issues, representing different physicians, medical associations, hospitals, and insurance companies. Numerous personal injury cases had taught me a great deal about medical care, treatment, medical business practices, and medical and insurance billings.

First, I disagreed that health insurance was a "right," as Obama had asserted (and President Clinton before him in 1992). But the Obama health-care plan itself seemed incorrect for the health-care crisis on many fronts. It did not address the rising costs of health care; did not address the failure in many areas of health care, such as infant mortality; and offered an unsustainable solution for the uninsured by expanding Medicaid. It didn't address the problem of malpractice lawsuits against physicians, which, according to a 2009 Gallup poll, may be responsible for as much as 26 percent of health-care cost. Beginning in January 2014, ObamaCare would massively expand Medicaid, making it available to any person under age sixty-five who falls below 133 percent of the federal poverty threshold. The law's goal is to give health care to an additional 32 million people and curtail the rising cost. We clearly had significant problems with our health-care system that needed to be addressed, but I did not think Congress had the authority to force Americans to purchase any product and fine them if they did not.

From a constitutional perspective, the passage of the health-care bill pushed me into the race. Although I certainly find that states have such authority, I do not think the federal government does. It seemed reckless, dangerous, and like political pandering, not to mention a waste of resources, to force such legislation through Congress. To me, this was an abominable way to handle such an important and serious issue. But other issues troubled me as well—particularly our economy and our national security. It seemed to me that we should consider how every issue—including health care—affects our economy and/or our national security.

Locally, I was very concerned about drilling for oil off the coast of Florida. In February—long before the Deepwater Horizon catastrophe wreaked havoc on the Gulf of Mexico—the Florida legislature was considering a bill that would remove the 125-mile limit for offshore drilling and allow oil companies to drill within three to ten miles of the Florida coastline. Early in my campaign, I addressed this as an environmental *and* economic issue, which it became when the BP oil spill caused such damage to the Gulf Coast.

Offshore drilling was one of the most important issues to the voters where I lived in South Walton. They cared less about party affiliation; they wanted to know where I stood on offshore drilling. In February, I posted this on the "Barbara for Congress" fan page on Facebook:

We cannot afford to take any action that would have a negative impact on our economy. We have the most beautiful beaches in the world and oil rigs in sight of our coastline would destroy our property values. Any oil spill would affect not only our natural resources but also our economy and way of life. It would hurt our tourism and our fishing industry, not to mention our military facilities and operations. This is not a matter we should even consider at this time.

As a woman approaching sixty, with twenty-six years of practicing law, I was a Republican because I believed in the basic principles of the party: less taxation, individual responsibility, and limited government. I did not believe then, nor do I believe now, that one party has all the answers.

But I thought my longtime friend Alex Castellanos might have an answer as to whether I should continue to pursue this race. Alex is the founder and owner of National Media, Inc., a public relations firm in Washington that provides consulting and media messaging to a conservative Republican clientele, like Bush 41 and 43, and, most recently, candidates for president Mitt Romney and John McCain. He is credited with the "soccer mom" ad campaign and called "father of the attack ad."

But more important to me, Alex is like family. When I first met Alex, I was in college and he was a sixteen-year-old lifeguard on the beach in Pine Knoll Shores in North Carolina. He later married my best friend, Susan Walton. She and I grew up in Jacksonville, North Carolina, and have been friends since we were little girls. I was Susan's maid of honor and am godmother to their two children. In early January, as other friends kept encouraging me to run for Congress, I called Alex for his opinion.

"I'm not a politician," I said.

"Good thing," he said, "Much easier for you to say you're not responsible for the mess we're in. You didn't vote for our excessive spending or for bankrupting the nation."

"But I don't really like politicians," I said.

"Who does?"

"I am not interested in a political career."

"First sign of an intelligent person. And perfect timing. Most people, especially now, don't like or trust politicians. Most people are not happy with the state of our nation. And they think politicians are responsible for the mess. I don't know if the District 2 seat is on the radar yet at the National Republican Congressional Committee, but they would love to have a serious candidate for this seat. We need smart people with integrity. We need people like you in Congress."

I was expecting more serious opposition from a seasoned political guru. I also expected more resistance from my Democratic friends. But what I found during this process was that everyone I spoke with said they wanted nonpartisan, nonpolitical people in Congress. I took them at their word, so I was both flattered and encouraged. But I knew that my lack of name recognition would probably diminish my ability to raise sufficient money for a congressional campaign.

Walton County had been my home since 2001. In the mid-1990s, I built a small beach house and drove 250 miles up and down Highway 331 and US I-65 to Birmingham most weekends. The weekends got longer and began to encroach into the week. Rather than leave the beach on Sunday afternoon, I left before dawn to be at my desk by 9:00 a.m. Then I began to squeeze an extra day at the end of the week by leaving late Thursday and arriving close to midnight. It was like being in love, but with a place, not a person.

In 2001, I closed my law practice, sold my home in Birmingham, and moved to Santa Rosa Beach in southern Walton County. I was fifty years old, and I wanted more adventure than the security of trying the same type of cases in the same courtrooms with the same lawyers for the next twenty years. It was a risk and felt like jumping from a train that had slowed down, but not stopped.

In the nine years since then, I have been involved in national class actions, such as *In re Managed Care*—the largest national class action at the time—where I worked with a team of lawyers who represented the physicians and medical associations against the billing and payment practices of insurance companies and their subsidiaries known as Health Management Organizations. I also worked with a team of lawyers to defend a major corporation against claims that its disposal of chemical pollutants had affected the health of individuals. I have consulted and testified as an expert witness on the payment practices of insurance companies and whether such practices were considered to be in bad faith. Aside from my lawyerly endeavors, my real-estate brokerage company has also kept me involved and busy.

Although a relative newcomer to Florida, I love Walton County, the Panhandle, the Gulf of Mexico, and life along 30-A, the county highway that runs along the Gulf. Just the southern part of the county that lies between the Chattahoochee Bay and the Gulf of Mexico is in Congressional District 2. The topography and demographics of this part of Walton County differs greatly from the northern part. The pristine white-sand beaches of South Walton are regularly called the most beautiful beaches in the world. The northern part is mostly tough hardscrabble country with little industry.

In 2010, District 2 was composed of sixteen counties ranging from the middle of Destin in the west to the state capital, Tallahassee, in the east, south to Apalachicola, and north to the Alabama state line. Geographically, it was one of the largest congressional districts. The westernmost counties were portions of Okaloosa, Walton, and Bay. The center counties included Jackson, Calhoun, Liberty, Gulf,

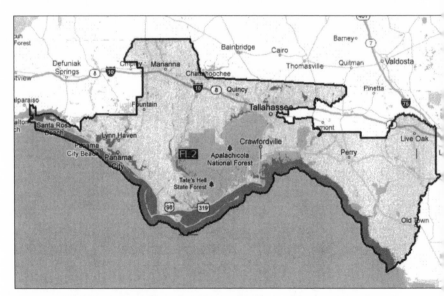

Detailed map of Florida District 2, showing the very small part of South Walton County in the district. In redistricting for 2012, Walton County is now one of six counties in Florida District 1. District 1 is talk-show host Joe Scarborough's former seat.

Franklin, Gadsden, Leon, and Wakulla. And the easternmost part of the district consisted of the counties of Jefferson, Taylor, Suwannee, Lafayette, and Dixie. (Redistricting in 2012 places Walton County in Congressional District 1, represented by Representative Jeff Miller, and formerly represented by talk-show host Joe Scarborough.)

Out of a population of 640,000 in 2010, 71 percent were white, 22 percent black, and 3 percent Hispanic—and the group was decidedly Democratic: 234,000 registered Democrats versus 158,657 registered Republicans. White male Democrats had occupied the congressional seat for most of the last 135 years, but it did not start out that way.

The first congressman to represent the district was a black Republican, a former slave, Josiah T. Walls. During the Reconstruction

The first congressman from Florida, Josiah T. Walls, was a Republican, a former slave who had served in both the Rebel and Union armies during the Civil War. Although he won three elections, he served only two terms in the House of Representatives; his white democratic Confederate opponents kept contesting his elections.

period after the Civil War, the Republican Party was deeply divided by the scalawags and carpetbaggers and chose Walls as the nominee to get the black vote and keep conservative Democrats from winning. After Walls, the seat went back and forth between the parties for a decade, but starting in 1885 it became solidly Democratic until James W. Grant won as a Democrat in 1986; he then switched his party affiliation to Republican in the middle of his second term and lost the subsequent election. Since then, it's been faithfully Democratic, with the incumbent Boyd winning the last seven elections.

So the odds of my winning the seat looked slim: only three Republicans had won the seat before, and never a woman. The only thing that appeared advantageous to me from a historical perspective was that I was white and a lawyer, but neither was of any real advantage: All the candidates in the 2010 Republican primary were white. And as I learned during the campaign, the general public's opinion of lawyers was very low in District 2.

I admit to a certain naïveté about America, its principles and its people. Despite the long odds, I thought I should run. I really believed that the groundswell of opposition to ObamaCare was indicative of the deep dissatisfaction with the agenda on the left and that someone like me could unseat the incumbent Democrat. But I underestimated the strength of the party's right wing, which would rekindle anti-intellectual sentiment, value culture over reason, and revive old fears of the national government that began with the Civil War—fears that were inextricably tied in the South to racial animosity, states' rights, and protecting the status quo of the establishment. I wasn't interested in protecting the establishment; I didn't think agendas helped make decisions; I didn't see the federal government as the enemy; and I thought we actually ought to be governed by the document on which the nation is founded, the Constitution. I was so out of step with the right wing of the party that I became a mere spectator to what amounted to a vulgar brawl.

3

Policy and Politics

Article I. Section. 8. Clause 1.

The Congress shall have Power to lay and collect Taxes, Duties, Imposts and Excises, to pay the Debts and provide for the common Defence and general Welfare of the United States; but all duties, imposts and excises shall be uniform throughout the United States.

As I began my search in January for the consultants, accountants, and fund-raisers I would need for the campaign, I interviewed many different people. One consultant team happened to be in Raleigh at the same time that I had come to North Carolina to discuss my plans with longtime friends and my ninety-two-year-old mother. I met the consultants at Winston's restaurant in the North Hills area of Raleigh for lunch.

I was met at the entrance by one of the consultants, who mentioned that she also suffered from knee problems. My knee would become more of an issue as the campaign went on, but early on, before the operation in April, I could still wear heels and walk without a limp. Chatting warmly, she and I walked back to a corner booth, where we could talk without intrusion. The senior consultant was waiting for us, sitting with his back to the wall. He was serious, direct, and friendly, but his voice was not southern. He had the direct manner of those born and bred north of the Mason-Dixon Line.

The senior consultant conducted the interview and handed me a copy of Newt Gingrich's book *Real Change*, saying he thought I might enjoy it. And I did: I found it to be an intelligent and thoughtful discussion of reasonable and practical solutions for our complex political problems. We discussed a number of issues that day, and I found the group bright, articulate, and personable, and I respected their opinions. They said they would accept one more candidate for 2010, and if I were interested, they would work with me. But as I was standing by my car as we parted, the senior consultant told me something I'll never forget. His voice was quiet but firm, and his gaze was level. "Barbara, this will be the hardest thing you'll ever do."

It felt prophetic, this utterance, and it made me nervous. I wanted to dismiss the foreshadowing of a hard truth, and I responded, "That may be, but I've been through some hard things before. I think I can get through this." The truth was, I could not imagine then the full extent of what they were telling me. The three of us thought a moderate, reasonable, intelligent approach to the campaign was the way to go. We set a deadline of March 31 for me to raise $150,000, at which point I would hire them. They also suggested, as had several others, that I travel to Washington to attend a candidate briefing conducted by the Heritage Foundation and meet with key members of the National Republican Congressional Committee (NRCC).

Prior to this, the only thing I knew about the Heritage Foundation was that it was a conservative think tank. Founded in 1973, the foundation is supported by private funding and listed as a nonprofit entity. The Board of Trustees are strong stalwarts of free enterprise, family privilege, personal accomplishments, and serious intellectual pursuits—Steve Forbes, publisher of *Forbes Magazine* and a presidential candidate in 1996 and 2000; Barb Van Andel-Gaby, daughter of Amway founder Jay Van Andel; and the conservatives' crown jewel, former British prime minister Margaret Thatcher, "Patron of the Heritage Foundation." In 2005, Thatcher chose the Heritage Foundation to house the Margaret Thatcher Center for Freedom. In an open letter to Heritage members, she noted that she looks to the foundation "to carry forward my legacy in the United States" because it is "an organization committed to defending and restoring sound conservative principles."

The Heritage Foundation in Washington, D.C. It was a cold, snowy day as I walked into this impressive building to be schooled on the important issues by Heritage fellows. I later learned the founder of the Heritage Foundation was responsible for targeting the "Moral Majority."

Heritage founder Paul Weyrich was a conservative activist who recruited money in the early 1970s from corporate magnates like Joseph Coors who were upset with the environmental restrictions on corporations passed after the first Earth Day in 1970. In the afterword of Barry Goldwater's book *The Conscience of a Conservative*, Robert Kennedy Jr. said the foundation was created "in order to formulate the philosophical underpinnings of an unholy alliance between big business and the ideological fanatics of the Christian right." Weyrich is generally credited with helping to launch the Moral Majority and the New Right of the Republican Party.

The Heritage is located along Massachusetts Avenue, down the street from Union Station and a few blocks from the Capitol. On the cold morning of March 3, I walked into the foundation through a side entrance because of exterior construction in the front. The furnishings inside were stock corporate—not overdone, with no impressive furniture, fabrics, or Oriental rugs. The familiar blue Heritage Foundation flags seen in the background of many televised speeches and press releases were displayed in the room I entered. My contact was a young twenty-something Scandinavian-looking young man named Landon Zinda. Landon had a quick wit and knew about my professional tennis career. He kept challenging me to a match, but I declined—I hadn't brought my racquet to Washington, after all; the recent knee injury and the forty-year age difference clearly were not considerations. Zinda took me to the second floor and walked me down a hallway past individual offices to a small conference room comfortably furnished with a bookcase, several Queen Anne upholstered chairs, and a round, dark table with six comfortable chairs. A large window facing Massachusetts Avenue filled the room with light. Coffee was available on a corner table.

"If it gets too crowded, we can move to another room," Landon told me. "Sometimes people come in, and if everyone enjoys themselves, they don't leave, and it can get crowded."

"I'm fine with crowded," I said. I was looking forward to this opportunity to engage with bright, smart, informed, and astute individuals on topics of vital importance to the country. But I wanted to set the pace. Sitting in a lecture taking notes is not my idea of an exhilarating encounter. If the pace is slow or the content boring, I lose interest. But tossing questions and answers back and forth like a spirited tennis match was more my "A game."

During the course of the day I met with the following Fellows and analysts: Nina Owcharenko (health care), Curtis Dubay (tax and economy), Ben Lieberman (energy), J. D. Foster (economy), James Phillips (Middle East affairs), and McKenzie Eaglen (national defense). All were extremely intelligent and impressive individuals, as one might expect.

I met first with J. D. Foster, a senior Heritage economist—a very astute man with a beard, a disciplined manner, and piercing eyes that seemed a perfect match for his laser-like mind. Initially, he leaned back in his chair, perhaps assessing the intellectual capacity of this congressional candidate. I tried to rein in my southern drawl, hoping not to be stereotyped. "I know that you are an expert in economics, and I am not, by a long shot. I listen better by asking questions—the lawyer in me, I guess. I know our time is limited. If we may, I would like to tell you what I think and have you tell me when I'm wrong, or by chance, if and when I'm correct." I smiled, and he returned a wary smile.

I told him I thought that the economy and national security were the two most critical issues. He nodded quietly. I suggested a freeze on spending, which he said was good, but would not help. I floated another economic solution—to cut discretionary spending—and he dismissed that as well. Looking to end this discouraging exchange, I asked, "Well, what is the answer?"

"The problem with the economy is our entitlements. Medicare, Medicaid, and Social Security take up 60 percent of the budget, and they're automatically increased every year. If we can't get a handle on those entitlements and change the way they're distributed, a massive wave of debt will overtake us. This is a hard truth for the American people, but without fixing this problem, we cannot fix the economic condition of this country. The sovereign debt is unsustainable and the amount of money that we have to borrow each year to meet our obligations to these programs is out of control. A crisis is coming."

Considering the dire nature of what he was telling me, he seemed very calm there in his dark suit. "What do you suggest?"

"We need to consider raising the eligibility age to over sixty-five years for Medicare and Social Security. And we need to seriously cut Medicare and Social Security benefits to those making over $150,000 per year in retirement income."

"In other words," I said somberly, "get the rich to give up what they have paid into the system for all these years, so that it will be available for others."

"Yes," Dr. Foster said directly. "That's the way it is."

"I can't see Republicans getting on board with this." Dr. Foster shrugged his shoulders. "Maybe so, but the numbers don't lie."

The data published by The Heritage Foundation show that if we don't curtail entitlements by the year 2050, every dollar of our tax revenue will go to funding those programs only, and we will not have so much as one dollar for a book, a bridge, or a bullet. But cutting entitlements is the 1,000-volt wire that no party or politician dares touch.

The debt crisis in Greece was discussed, and I asked Dr. Foster if

Entitlement Spending

- Entitlement spending is on autopilot, with annual spending determined by benefit formulas and caseloads.
- Entitlements (excluding net interest) account for 65 percent of all federal spending and a record 18 percent of GDP. Even if all financial bailouts were excluded, the remaining 13 percent of GDP spent on entitlement programs would still be a record.
- Nominal entitlement spending (excluding bailouts) is projected to nearly double over the next decade.
- The President's health care initiative would substantially expand entitlement spending.
- The three largest entitlements are Social Security, Medicare, and Medicaid. Their total cost is projected to leap from 8.4 percent of GDP in 2007 to 18.6 percent by 2050.
- Unless Social Security, Medicare, and Medicaid are reformed, policymakers will eventually have to choose from among:
  - Raising taxes by the current equivalent of $12,072 per household by 2050, and further thereafter;
  - Eliminating every federal program except Social Security, Medicare, and Medicaid; or
  - Increasing the national debt to unprecedented levels that could cause an economic collapse.

Three Major Entitlements Will Absorb All Taxes by 2050

Percentage of Gross Domestic Product, by Fiscal Year

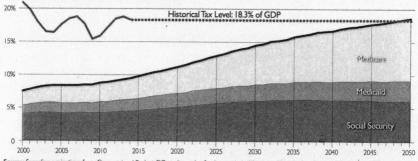

Source: Spending projections from Congressional Budget Office, alternative fiscal scenario in "The Long-Term Budget Outlook," December 2007.

Tax Increase Needed to Fund Social Security, Medicare, and Medicaid Cost Increases

Tax Increase per Household, Adjusted for Inflation and Income Growth (2009)

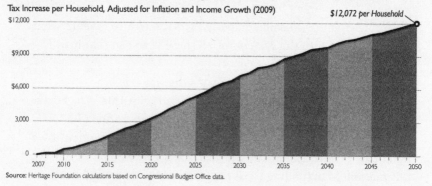

$12,072 per Household

Source: Heritage Foundation calculations based on Congressional Budget Office data.

Chart produced by the Heritage Foundation showing that the three major entitlement programs will absorb all taxes in the year 2050. Two years after my race, a new Heritage Foundation chart showed that all tax revenues will be absorbed by entitlements by 2045.

America was headed in the same direction and how soon we might get there. He answered calmly, "Of course, I don't know. But I wouldn't be surprised if we were in such an economic predicament in twelve to eighteen months. We must get a handle on both our national debt and our deficit. There is already a great deal of talk about reducing the United States' bond ratings."

As Landon predicted, people had fun and didn't leave after their appointed times, and it became an intellectual free-for-all, with me receiving all the benefit. There did not seem to be a second to move to a larger, more comfortable room. We sat in this small room with a half dozen or so Heritage Fellows, only moving for coffee or a sandwich that was brought in, while issues swirled around us.

We discussed taxes, and it was suggested there should be tax cuts for those earning less than $250,000 a year. Some thought that the value-added tax was next on Obama's agenda and would plunge us into a further economic crisis. We discussed the current health-care bill and the alternative plans the country could afford. We discussed defense spending, the age of our planes, and the proposed reduction in ships that would shrink our Navy to less than it was in 1916.

I wanted to discuss Iran, and, especially nuclear weapons and the relationship between Israel and Iran. This proved to be one of the most interesting discussions as Jim Phillips, the Heritage's Middle East expert, was extremely informative. I had forgotten that Eisenhower's "Atoms for Peace" program permitted the shah of Iran to have a nuclear reactor provided by the United States in return for a nonproliferation agreement. And, of course, that the current regime did not recognize the authority of that treaty. On that very day, Israel had released a photograph of its latest drone the size of a 747—an obvious statement of Israel's strength and determination.

The only time I noted a partisan attitude was when we discussed offshore drilling. I told Ben Lieberman that Florida currently had a 125-mile buffer in place, and that I thought we needed more safeguards for the environment prior to allowing companies to drill closer to shore. I was asked to at least allow each district to decide for itself on this issue. And while I acknowledged that that generally would be my position, I said, "Well, what if the district next door, or another state allows offshore drilling and there is a spill that ultimately damages my district?" On that point, we had to agree to disagree. The Deepwater Horizon oil spill answered that question, at least in the short term.

It was an interesting day at the Heritage. Despite my constitutional concerns, I came away understanding that the state of the economy was the single-most critical issue we face. I decided that the economy should be the focus of my campaign, including the entitlement programs and the solutions needed to remedy the deficit.

The focus on the campaign trail, however, proved to be the "evilness" of the current administration, the Mexicans, abortion, gay marriage, gay adoption, and the Muslims and their mosques. Instead of hearing articulate discussions about our problems, I would hear generic Tea Party refrains of: "We're not going to take it anymore!," "Let's take our country back!," and "Have you had enough?"

I knew, of course, that these ultra-right issues were important to many Republicans. I did not fully appreciate that social issues—and the demand for a prescribed ideological response to them—could trump all other issues. When I left D.C. in March 2010, I thought that when the voters truly understood the facts, they would put aside their differences on smaller matters to deal with the more critical issues.

I would come to that debate—and debacle—soon enough, but Alex had said, "Jump in. The water's fine." The temperature at the Heritage had felt pretty good. I didn't know that I'd get boiled.

•

The following morning, I met with the staff at the NRCC and later talked to the committee's chairman, Texas congressman Pete Sessions, and the House minority whip, Virginia congressman Eric Cantor. Cantor cofounded the Young Guns Program in the 2008–8 election cycle with Paul Ryan and Kevin McCarthy in order to defeat incumbent Democrats. When four Young Guns won, Sessions adopted the program for the recruitment and training of the NRCC's most promising Republican House candidates. Outside the Young Guns Program, the NRCC also provides research and direct financial contributions to candidates.

The policy free-for-all at the Heritage had been an exhilarating intellectual experience, but the NRCC was all about politics and money. As an accomplished lawyer, I had successfully navigated hundreds if not thousands of motion arguments, trials, and appellate arguments. Because the primary function of Congress is to pass laws, I thought that education and experience would be an asset in running for Congress, and that rational thoughtfulness would be the norm. My meetings with Representatives Cantor and Sessions were the first indications of my naïveté about politics.

That morning I met with a number of young NRCC staff members—young men who specialized in field research, finance, issue research, and media contacts. Ben Cassidy was my liaison, and I worked with Andy Sere, regional press secretary; Tim Garron, regional political director; Joe Sciarrino, new media strategist; Jon Black, director of research; Tom Prewitt, field research analyst; and Trent Edwards, director of field finance. In the early afternoon, my Young Guns liaison for the day guided me through labyrinthine tunnels toward Cantor's office in the Cannon House Office Building. It was a cold, snowy, and blustery day, and I was still wearing my camel overcoat and scarf as we sat for a few minutes in Cantor's office chatting with the receptionist. When we were ushered toward Cantor's office, Cantor met us at the door. I was surprised by his light build and frame as he reached out his hand. He seemed so young that I started to call him "Eric," but caught myself and said, "Congressman, so good of you to meet with me." He smiled thinly and moved to his chair, two of his staff members quietly taking seats beside him as my guide and I found our seats on the silk downstuffed couch. Although Cantor was the minority whip, it honestly seemed as if we had nothing to discuss. I am sure it was not helpful that I was more interested in policy than politics, and both the atmosphere and the conversation were formal and restrained. The meeting was fairly brief and touched on nothing substantive until I was about to leave.

Cantor sat on the edge of his Queen Anne chair, while his staffers lounged back deep into their chairs, silent and looking as if they anticipated deadly boredom. At one point, Cantor raised his hand to the knot in his bright-blue club tie and pretended to straighten it. He tilted his head slightly to the right as he said, "I understand that you're a tennis player," and smiled, ever so thinly. "Perhaps we should have a match. I was quite the player in high school." Inwardly, I rolled my eyes.

I smiled, but before I could respond, my young guide said, "Congressman, Barbara played *professional* tennis." Cantor shook his head in a patrician manner to indicate the invitation was withdrawn. "I didn't know that. I didn't realize."

I interjected a southern face-saving response. "Well, you have age on your side and I have had quite a few injuries."

"Still, you would be way out of my league," he said. He laughed lightly as he stood. "I expect to see you here next January after you've won the general election," he said, holding out his hand.

I shook his hand and said, "Thank you, sir, that's very kind of you." I assumed his prediction was just southern graciousness.

He leveled his gaze at me and said, "We only have seventeen Republican women serving in the House. We need more smart Republican women in Congress. We need women like you." (In 2010, there were sixty-one Democratic women in the House, and although the numbers improved slightly for the 111th Congress, Democratic women still outnumber Republican women three to one.)

My guide had scheduled the last meeting of the day with Representative Pete Sessions, chairman of the NRCC, the headquarters of which is located in a standard-issue gray corporate building at 320 First Street, S.E., a block from Cantor's office. There had been too many meetings since Cantor, and as the meeting with Sessions was going to be delayed, I told my guide that I would just "beg off" and "take a rain check." But he was adamant that I wait and meet with Sessions. He assured me this was a meeting that "I could not miss."

Sessions made several unsuccessful bids for Congress before he won in 1997. In one unsuccessful bid in 1993, Sessions made a tour of his district with a livestock trailer full of horse manure, claiming that the Clintons' health-care plan stunk more than the horse manure. Sessions is not a large man, but his energy and presence filled the doorway as he extended a hand and led me into his office. His handshake was warm and enthusiastic as he instructed me in a rapid-fire staccato to place my winter coat and bag in a specific chair. I turned to my left, setting them in the chair as instructed. As I turned back, I felt a strong hand around my shoulder. "Smile," he said as I turned to find his secretary aiming a camera at us from five feet away. The flash caught me looking surprised, like a squirrel caught in headlights.

We had a spirited conversation, discussing money, consultants, and both the importance and difficulty of a first-time victory. During the meeting he said, "I put in $200,000 of my own money the first time I ran and lost. How much are you planning to put in?" I am not a wealthy person, so my response was: "I was thinking somewhere south of that figure." Sessions questioned me about consultants, and asked my guide who would be the best one for me. He demanded that my guide provide the best consultant to work with me, although neither one of us thought that was his responsibility. We exchanged glances and nodded.

Sessions made it clear he did not like Republicans engaging in public fighting during a campaign. He said, "I don't want to hear about any fighting going on down there among any of our people— do you understand what I'm saying?" I nodded. "I hear about any fighting among the candidates down in Florida, and I'm going to come down there, you hear me?" Again, I thought nodding the best response, as I noticed Sessions had a tendency to repeat himself, as if I weren't paying attention. Believe me, I was.

He got up from the round table where we were sitting and walked to the doorway and hollered several times for his assistant. A young woman with a bright smile handed him a sheet of paper. He walked back, sat down, and slid the paper to me, as he said, "Know what this is? Do you know?"

"Yes," I said, "I am aware of this."

"It's the Taxpayer Protection Plan," he responded, reading the words at the top of the page. "Yes," I said, somewhat drolly, "I know."

"Have you signed it yet? Have you signed it?" "No, I have not," I said.

"Erica! Erica!" he bellowed to the empty doorway, and when she failed to appear within a nanosecond, he pushed himself out of his chair and to the doorway, almost bumping into Erica as she entered the room.

"The camera," Sessions said. "Get the camera."

I cut my eyes to my young guide who was grinning from ear to ear, clearly enjoying himself. Sessions returned to the table as he instructed me to wait for Erica before signing.

With Congressman Pete Sessions, chairman of the National Republican Congressional Committee, in March 2010. This is a picture of me doing something that I would later regret: signing the Taxpayer Protection Pledge. Our candidates have to be strong in refusing to sign pledges that undermine our intellectual integrity.

"Well, I have some concerns about this—" Sessions cut me off.

"You don't believe in higher taxes, do you?" "No, generally, I do not." He continued, "Then you have to sign it—that's all there is to it." I had some concerns about signing such a pledge, but at the time, I was more focused on the "marginal rates" portion of the pledge and did not find that to really be significant in the overall tax code issues. Later, I would regret ever signing any pledge.

Toward the end of our meeting, he got up and walked to his desk. He picked up a blue Sharpie and wrote on a business card. Then he came back, sat down next to me, and handed me two cards—his "Member of Congress" card and his NRCC chairman card. He tapped the NRCC card where he had written his e-mail address in liberty blue. With his close-cropped gray hair, steely-blue eyes, and trim physique, he had the bearing of a former military officer, which he was not. He was, however, an Eagle Scout.

His gaze was direct and intense as he continued tapping the card. "Here is my private. E-mail. OK? This comes directly. To my Blackberry. I want you to call me. Before you do anything. Stupid. Do you hear me?"

He jabbed at the e-mail address with a pointed index finger and repeated, "You understand what I'm saying?" I could not tell whether we were in a bad rerun of *Hogan's Heroes,* or I had been conscripted somewhere along the way into the Boy Scouts. I knew I was supposed to reply earnestly, "Yes, sir!" But I just could not do it.

Instead, I said, "So you think I'll realize that I'm about to do something stupid, but will need to call you so I don't actually go forward and do something stupid. Do I have that right?" If I had known about his former horse-manure campaign stunt, I would not have been able to resist saying, "So, for example, would pulling a trailer load of horse manure be a smart or stupid thing?"

Sessions's unblinking intensity was fixed upon me as if he had not gotten through to me. He gave a slight shake of his head and blew a puff of air through his nostrils, as one does before repeating something exactly—but this time more loudly and slowly, as if changing volume and pace would get it through. "Anything stupid. Before. You do. Anything stupid." He kept punctuating his words while tapping his card like I needed direction on where to look and he had to help me focus my attention. "You need. To call me. (*Tap, tap*) Or. E-mail. Me. (*Tap, tap*) Got it? (*Tap*) Under. Stand?" (*Tap, tap, tap*)

I realized I was not going to get out of this eddy of stupidity unless I acquiesced. It had been a long day, it was late, and I was anxious to leave. "Yes, I think I've got it. Anything stupid, call you first." Sessions nodded curtly as my guide stifled a laugh and tried to cover it with a cough. Sessions looked back and forth between the two of us, hesitating for a moment before deciding that we were finished. He gave a mission-accomplished nod and stood up satisfied. We shook hands, and as we left, he closed the door to his office.

I was shaking my head and laughing as we walked down the hallway from Sessions's office. My guide's face was red with mirth as he said, "That was great. I've never seen anybody handle Pete like that. The last women candidate he met with slapped him."

"Really? I'm beginning to understand why there are so few Republican women in Congress. So, some woman candidate actually slapped him?" My guide stifled a guffaw as he nodded. "Oh my gosh, that seems a little over the top." We both laughed. I found the whole encounter humorous, if somewhat disconcerting.

I couldn't help wondering if Sessions made the "stupid" statement to all candidates or just to the female candidates? I couldn't imagine him giving the same advice to a man. Maybe he wasn't sexist and he said that to every candidate. It was, to me, clearly bizarre behavior, of which I was seeing more and more as I got further into this race. I could not imagine suggesting that someone I had just met might "do something stupid." It seemed an odd way to win friends and influence people, but then, as I have said, I was new to politics.

It was late, cold, and rainy when my friend Susan picked me up for dinner outside the NRCC after my meeting with Sessions. I was weary as I tried to explain my day. As we drove to Alexandria, a relative called to ask me to help negotiate the legal issues surrounding his marital dispute. I listened as long as I could, providing my best legal advice while thinking of a nice glass of wine and some much-needed laughter to relax.

At the end of the day, I kept coming back to Eric Cantor's earnest statement about the small number of Republican women serving in Congress. And I remembered that a woman had never been elected from my district. The odds against me seemed to be mounting, but at that time, I was still oblivious to the real odds.

4

The Headquarters

Article I. Section 8.

Congress shall have Power . . . To regulate Commerce
with foreign Nations, and among the several States.

After the chilly weather and meetings in Washington, I was eager to get home and begin the actual campaign. One of the things I love best about flying home to Walton County is looking out over the bright-turquoise waters of the Gulf of Mexico, the deeper blue-green Choctawhatchee Bay, and the emerald-green waters of St. Andrews Bay. Once on the ground, I was looking forward this time to seeing friends, getting in a game of tennis, and maybe some early-spring waterskiing if the temperature allowed. But the first thing I did was to go to Modica Market, an Italian grocery store, and see what was going on in Seaside, which is all of six blocks from my house.

Seaside is a planned beachside cottage community that harkens back to a place and time where we never lived but our parents and grandparents did—a town where you can walk to the market, the post office, and restaurants, with stops along the way to chat with neighbors on their front porches. Modica Market was my unofficial campaign headquarters. The locals and summer residents coming in day and night provided a ready mix of people to engage with on the current political event of the day. I would spend an hour or so

Modica Market located in Seaside, Florida. My unofficial campaign headquarters was in this fabulous Italian market, where I would visit with voters and talk politics. It is the actual heart of Seaside.

there a day when I had time, meeting and talking with people. I loved hearing about their concerns, no matter where they were from or their party affiliation. Many people in this affluent area have second homes, and although they spend a part of the year in Georgia, Tennessee, Texas, or Arkansas, they are registered voters in Florida.

Most grocery stores in the Panhandle specialize in Budweiser, boiled peanuts, and white Bunny bread. In contrast, Modica Market has Old World charm, genteel sophistication, an upscale palate, and a blue-collar work ethic. It is rather like a grocery-store version of the television show *Cheers*. Not only do they know your name there, but you can also make a credit arrangement and they will know your number. Children who can barely reach the counter know the magic number to their parents' account that allows them to leave with candy, Coke, or chicken nuggets. You can certainly buy the basics, like eggs and milk, but also all sorts of exotic European cookies, olive oils, and fine bottles of wine. Should you want to, you can also participate in the sense of family at Modica—chatting with Charles Modica Sr., his wife, Sara, or son, Charles Jr. about food, wine, Italy, or daily events. People come back all day long, sometimes a half dozen times or more. They pretend they need this or that or forgot this or that, but what the Modica family is really selling and what people want is something you can't purchase. And so people show up for another jar of olives, candles for a birthday cake, a smile, a glass of wine, an exchange of pleasantries, a feeling of belonging.

And like others, when I moved to the Panhandle, I began to gravitate not only toward the grocery store but also toward this warm and wonderful family. I would come to Modica for coffee, or a beer, or espresso beans, or conversation with friends. Standing at the end of the counter while Charles Jr. waited on customers, he and I would have a chance to chat about the day. As one of my very best friends, I had talked with him prior to running. He was concerned about the toll it might take on me financially and physically, but said he could not think of a "better person" to be in Congress. When I decided to run, his family gave me their full support.

Modica Market has an impressive clientele, with many successful individuals having a summer home in Seaside or the surrounding area known as "30-A." Either Charlie or Charles Senior would introduce me to people they thought I should know, many of whom followed and supported my campaign. Charles Senior was never shy about telling people to contribute. The market was where I first met David Flannery.

It was a blustery winter day, and Charlie and I were drinking hot espresso. A middle-aged, average-sized man with Yellow Oakley sun-

Seaside's Anchor

Charlie Modica met his competition head-on, shifting focus and giving his customers a unique experience

BY JOHN VAN GIESON

Charles Modica Jr. and Modica Market. Charlie was concerned about the physical and financial toll the campaign would have on me, but once I decided to run, he and his sweet daddy, Charles Sr., were a rock of support.

glasses perched on his head and another pair of glasses resting on his nose came through the line. "Mr. Flannery," Charlie said warmly. "Do you two know each other? Because you should." Mr. Flannery pressed his lips together and wrinkled his nose as he looked down through his glasses. "No!" he said shortly.

I smiled and extended my hand. "I don't think so. I'm Barbara Olschner."

"Oh, hey," Mr. Flannery said, shifting his drink and muffin to the other hand as he shook my hand. I thought I detected a northern accent.

"Miss Barbara is running for Congress," Charlie said with pride. "Y'all should really know each other."

"Really? Which party?"

"Does it really matter?" I said.

He suppressed a guffaw-giggle. "Well, yes, actually, it does."

"Well, I am running as a Republican, but I don't think any one party has it right."

Mr. Flannery shook his head as if trying to shake that notion. "Well, one has it more right than the other. I'm a Democrat. There has never been a Republican I could support."

I decided the abrasive accent must be from New Jersey. "And you don't have to, although there are a lot of Democrats supporting me. I don't think it matters which party is in control if our problems are solved with reason and intellect."

Mr. Flannery nodded. He shuddered like he had a chill, which could have been the wind and rain, or the conversation. "Well, that's nice, but I'm not one of those Democrats."

"I don't have to have every vote. And everybody won't be able to support me." I thought this would be the end of it.

He hesitated before the door. "So what made you run?"

"Health care. I know a lot about health-care issues because of my legal practice, and even if you were in favor of universal health care, which I am not, this is clearly a disaster."

Mr. Flannery pushed his sunglasses farther back on his head. "Yeah, there are some problems with it, for sure. I know a lot about health care too. That was my business until I retired."

"Oh, then I'm sure we could have an interesting conversation."

"Well, too bad you're in the wrong party. My hand, my family, my Catholic guilt, my brain wouldn't let me write a check to a Republican. Sorry, too bad."

"Well, you could always vote for one."

Mr. Flannery shuddered, and this time I knew it was not the weather. "Oh, eck, no, never. That would be worse."

"Well, the great thing about this country is that it works best when we all follow our conscience. And it's nice to know you will do that. Glad to meet you."

"Yeah, better luck next election." Mr. Flannery blustered out into the blustery day.

I looked at Charlie incredulously. "You thought I should meet that guy?"

Charlie shrugged and smiled. "Very smart and very accomplished guy. But he can be a bit of an ass."

"You think?" I said, and we laughed.

The next day Charlie called me. "Remember that guy you met yesterday?"

"The Yankee guy?"

"Yeah! He wants your number. Said he wants to talk with you. He said he was impressed with the way you handled yourself."

"Really?"

The day after, Mr. Flannery and I met at a table in the back of Modica Market, drinking coffee and talking about politics, health care, and my congressional race. He did not seem as raw as on that rainy, windy day, although his complexion was ruddy. He was bright and engaging.

"Thank you for meeting with me," said David Flannery.

"Thank you for contacting me."

"I was impressed with how you handled me. I can be an ass sometimes."

I smiled. "Well, can't we all? This political climate has everyone on both sides in a perpetual bad mood. But we have serious problems, and being polarized and angry with the other side is not going to help, but it will hurt. I've settled lawsuits my whole life, and I know that you don't get anywhere calling names and pitching a fit. You have to be able to work with logic and reason, examine both sides, and reach a result."

"Well," said Flannery, "You would be a breath of fresh air in the Republican Party. Hell, in any party. Are there any important local issues that will affect this campaign?"

"Yes," I said. "Offshore drilling. People are pretty upset over it, and I'm against it, for economic and environmental reasons, even though the Republican party line is pro-drilling."

"Well, I like anything that is against the GOP party line, but I don't see this being an important issue," Flannery said, drinking his latte.

"It's very important to the voters here, and that makes it an important issue, although I agree with you that it's a state issue. But it could be very important for the voters," I said, not realizing at the time that BP was about to dump massive amounts of oil in the Gulf. A seasoned local politician had brought this issue to my attention when I had been deciding whether to run. I had been told I needed to know where I stood on this early, and I had researched it. I took this person's advice and was glad that I did.

"I don't see it," said Flannery with a clipped tone. "It's a nonissue. So what are your thoughts about health care?"

"Let me start by saying that a great deal of my knowledge comes from a national class action on behalf of all the physicians and medical associations against the Health Management Organizations. I was on a team of lawyers representing the docs. Knowing a good bit about insurance, billings and payments, fee for service, and how that whole system works, I think the employer-based system is outdated—inefficient, ineffective, and much too expensive for what it provides. Despite all the resources devoted to health care, it is really a flawed system, no matter how you view it. It has failed to contain cost and it has failed to improve quality. Look at where we rank with other countries on longevity or infant mortality."

Flannery nodded thoughtfully. "Exactly. What are we 'reforming?' Neither party, nor President Obama, has clearly articulated that, and most people don't or can't distinguish between the systemic delivery of health care and the traditional roles of health insurance companies. The average citizen is all for 'reforming' health insurance, prohibiting the exclusion of preexisting conditions, limiting increases in premiums, and reducing the administrative paperwork hassles associated with health insurance plans. That same citizen understands very little about the deeply embedded and systemic flaws in the health-care system itself. No real effort has been made to contain the actual cost of the services provided. There's little in the way of quality assurance, and never a 'money-back guarantee.'"

I jumped in. "Well, that's why this makes no sense to me, this

Obama health-care bill. I don't think we've addressed the real issues. Instead, we've pushed through something for political reasons. We can't reform a system that is completely broken by adding 32 million more people to it."

Flannery pushed back the glasses on his nose. "But you know who is currently insuring these 30, 40, 50 million people, whatever the number is, don't you?"

"Yes, I do—the taxpayers."

Flannery cut in and completed my thoughts. "And in the most inefficient, inequitable, and nontransparent way possible."

"You know, I'm not sure it is realistic to think we can insure everyone," I said. "But there are things that can be done to make insurance more available and affordable. For example, we know that the premiums on catastrophic insurance are relatively inexpensive. If our goal is to provide basic care for everyone, then perhaps we should look at state or private clinics that could provide the most basic care and educate people about catastrophic policies for those injuries or illnesses that could bankrupt them. Just a thought."

"Are you sure you're a Republican?"

"Pretty sure," I said. "I just think if we would use less political jargon and accusatory language, we could solve many of these problems. There is a distinction between trying to solve a problem and whether there is authority under the Constitution for a federal solution. I don't see that Congress had the power under the Constitution to force everyone to purchase a product and then fine those who do not participate. If you look at the powers enumerated to Congress under Article I, Section 8, you would have to find the authority for ObamaCare under the power to 'regulate commerce,' and I don't think the courts will extend it that broadly. But the states certainly have the authority to enact health-care reform."

"I don't think any legal argument is going to be that important in your race, but can I help you on any of these issues? I participated in the first health-care debate—on Hillary's side, of course. And I'm impressed with you and will contribute to your campaign. You're smart, no question. But you're not as smart as Hillary."

I couldn't help laughing at this guy. "Well, it's early in the campaign. You might change your mind."

He shook his head, smiling. "No, I don't think so. Not about that. Sorry."

"No need to be." I stood up. "I'm not trying to be the smartest. I'm just trying to make the best contribution I can."

I stayed at Modica after Flannery left. I bought a beer and milk and went through the checkout line manned by Charles Senior. He was the picture of an Italian grocer, with his neatly trimmed white beard, his pressed shirt and white apron. As he rang up my items, he raised his white eyebrows and said, "How did that go?"

"Very well, Mr. Charles. We had a good conversation."

"And?"

"He's going to contribute."

"Very good!" said Mr. Charles with a big smile. "Big check?"

"That's what he says!"

"Good job," said Mr. Charles, clearly delighted for me.

Mr. Charles put my milk in a bag, and as I reached for it, he lightly touched my arm and almost under his breath, and with kindness, he said, "You're a good lady." Before I could get teary, he said, "Now, go have a wonderful evening."

This was not the first time he'd told me I was a good lady, but it never failed to surprise me and fill me with pride and gratitude. It meant more to me than he could know. Mr. Charles passed away while I was working on this book.

5

Two New Candidates

Article V

The Congress, whenever two-thirds of both Houses shall deem
it necessary, shall propose Amendments to this Constitution,
or, on the Application of the Legislatures of two-thirds of
the several States, shall call a Convention for proposing
Amendments, which, in either Case, shall be valid to all Intents
and Purposes, as Part of this Constitution, when ratified by
the Legislatures of three-fourths of the several States, or by
Conventions in three-fourths thereof, as the one or the other
Mode of Ratification may be proposed by the Congress.

The resort development at Bluewater Bay is a section of Okaloosa County north of Choctawhatchee Bay, but part of Congressional District 2. Of the sixteen counties in the district, the three in the western part of the district are divided counties—part of the county is in District 1 and part is in District 2. Because Democrats so outnumber Republicans in my district, I felt I had to approach the Republicans in this small resort area frequented mostly by retired military and young families needing close access to Eglin Air Force Base and Northwest Regional Airport. The resort at Bluewater Bay sports a 120-slip marina, a 21-court tennis facility, and a 36-hole Tom Fazio/Jerry Pate–designed golf course. Many of the amenities take advantage of the beautiful view of Choctawhatchee Bay framed by moss-covered oak trees.

On the night of March 15, the local women's Republican Federated Club of Okaloosa County hosted the candidate forum in the dining room of the Bluewater Bay Golf Club. The furnishings were a little worn—not unusual for a public golf course. About twenty-five people milled about the room, speaking to candidates and to each other. They were neither rundown beach folk nor millionaires; they were retired military with an earnest Midwest connection. If you were still in the range of forty years old, you were one of the younger gals in this club. Dinner was ten dollars and was either chicken or fish, although both looked and tasted the same. The candidates' brochures, bumper stickers, and buttons covered a table at the back of the room.

A long table at the front of the room was arranged for the candidates—of whom there were now six, with five in attendance. Eddie Hendry, the salesman, and Steve Southerland, the undertaker, were both there, but Charlie Ranson, the dignified lawyer, did not appear. I was no longer in the shadows about my candidacy. And there were two new candidates: David Scholl and Dianne Berryhill.

David was forty-eight years old, married, and living in Bluewater

Flier for candidate David Scholl. David first said he was in the Air Force for twenty-eight years and had been a Delta pilot for twenty years. Because he was only forty-eight years old, voters began to question his math. His later fliers reflected that he had been in the Reserves for a majority of that time.

Bay. He said he had had a twenty-eight-year career in the Air Force and had been a Delta pilot for twenty years. When voters began to question his math, he said he had been in the Air Force Reserves while flying for Delta. David is not tall, but he has great posture, probably from his military service. Sometimes even his hair seemed to stand at attention. He smiled and laughed all the time and had an abundance of energy. The first time I met him, David was so excited and pleased about marching in Reagan's inaugural parade that you would have thought it had just happened yesterday—he mentioned it in every speech. He said he was running for Congress because Representative Boyd's vote for cap and trade legislation would cause David to lose his job as a commercial pilot—although he never explained why. When he wanted to make a point, he would stand perched on the end of his toes, roll forward, and jab with his fist: "Since Boyd came after my job" (*roll-jab*), "I decided to go after his!"

That night at Bluewater, David was so energized that he bounced up from his chair whenever it was his turn to speak. And several times he seemed so happy to be there that he laughed before he had even said anything.

I knew that Dianne Berryhill was a candidate because the names of all candidates were posted online and also because she had called me at home one night in early February. It was about 9:00 p.m., and she introduced herself and said she would like to schedule a time for me to speak at an upcoming Republican meeting in Tallahassee at the Capital City Club. Then she started probing: "I see that you're a lawyer."

"Yes," I said, thinking it a little odd for one candidate to call another candidate directly.

"And you live in Walton County, right? Do you live on the beach? I see that you're a real-estate broker too."

I was quiet as I rolled my eyes.

"Have you ever been in politics before?" she asked, most politely.

Thinking this was unusual behavior but being new to politics, I said, "Aren't you a candidate too?"

"Oh, yes," she said, "but I am the president and founder of the blah blah blah. . . ."

It was late and I have never been that impressed with titles, so some of what she said I can't remember. She talked for such a long time—and said such outlandish things—that I began to think she must be sucking down white wine with a straw. She really didn't engage in a conversation: she made statements and I just listened.

"My husband, Don, and I have a perfect family. I have started

CONTRACT WITH THE PEOPLE

I WILL SUPPORT LEGISLATION THAT ENDORSES:
Right To Life
Lower Taxes
Right To Bear Arms
Strong National Security
Freedom Of Speech
Finding And Ending Fraud, Waste And Abuse
Limiting Government Programs
Limiting The Influence Of Lobbyists, and
Increasing The Influence Of The People
Sound Energy Policy
Protection Of Our Borders
Conservative Values

I WILL NEVER VOTE ON ANY BILL WITHOUT
ASKING THE FOLLOWING QUESTIONS:
Is It Right/ Moral?
Is It Constitutional?
Is It Necessary?
Is It Affordable?
How Do The People Of My District Want Me To Vote?

I PROMISE TO TERM LIMIT MYSELF TO SERVIING
ONLY 8 YEARS. I PROMISE TO HONOR THE
PEOPLE'S VOICES THAT I REPRESENT, AND TO
NEVER FORGET THAT I AM A REPRESENTATIVE
OF THE PEOPLE FIRST AND A DC
CONGRESSWOMAN SECOND.

EARLY VOTE AUGUST 9TH-21ST, 2010

Flier for candidate Dianne Berryhill with her "Contract with the People." She kept asking me to sign it, always in front of an audience.

this that and the other Republican club. I grew up in politics. I know pretty much everybody in the Republican Party. We are very financially sound. I have been an accountant, a designer, a mother, wife, and Indian chief"—or something like that.

"We have a son in the military—we are so proud of him. He is stationed overseas. My daughters are in law school—both of them. We are just the perfect American family—did I mention that?

"Don't you *hate* Michael Steele? You *don't*? How can you *not* hate what he has done to the Republican Party? I'm very well connected in Republican circles. I started the Capital Conservative Consistent City Cornucopia Republican Club"—I am making up some of the C-words, but there were a lot of them.

"So, why *are* you in this race? Sounds to me like someone just talked you into it?" I thought that was interesting since I'd hardly said a thing.

"So . . . you're a lawwwwyer," she said in her best Cruella De Vil voice. "I think we've got plenty of them in Washington, and we don't need any more. You know, people don't like lawyers."

I wondered how long this would go on. I was trying to be polite, but it was becoming more difficult. She took a deep breath as if drawing on a cigarette and continued trying to convince me to drop out of the race. "Well, I'm sure you're a nice person. But it takes more than that. I guess you just did this on a whim? Sounds to me like you got talked into this. You won't be in the race for long."

At this point I decided the conversation was over. "Make no mistake, Denise . . ."

"Dianne."

"Right," I said in a steely tone. "I am a very serious candidate for Congress. I have a real understanding of the issues we are facing, and I am not in this for some political junket. We need competent, qualified, and educated leaders in Washington able to tackle serious issues, and that is why I am in this race." There was a fumble and a click before Dianne and I were disconnected. But the late-night calls continued from the only other female in the race.

So at Bluewater Bay, I was finally able to put a face to the late-night voice on the other end of the phone line. Dianne was a petite woman who didn't look like she'd borne five children. Dianne's husband, Don, was with her that night. Don was always very person-able to all the candidates and had a very engaging smile and robust handshake. He was there in full support of his wife, ready to carry signs or buttons or wave and grin. She was dressed very nicely, but conservatively, in a skirt and blouse like she was on her way home from church. Her hair was frosted, sprayed, and neatly in place, and her makeup was artfully applied.

That night Dianne was fairly subdued as she answered questions, but she asked me again if I was dropping out of the race. She even called me a few more times at home to ask the same question until I stopped answering her calls. Every time I saw her at a public gather-ing, she would trip up to me in her straight skirt and strappy heels and look me straight in the eye as she said, "What are *you* doing here?" As she did this at every gathering, I grew tired of responding, "I'm in the race," and would just smile at her. She would finally get around to the question that was really on her mind: "When are you dropping out?"

In early April, I hurt my left knee playing tennis. This same knee had been reworked in the early 1970s, and after that surgery I had played professional tennis. But from time to time, over the years, my knee would give me trouble. This injury in April seemed worse than before, and when I went to the ski lake the following day, I could not put my left leg in the back binding in my slalom ski. I went straight to the MRI—wet hair and all—which indicated a torn meniscus both medial and laterally. Within a week I was in Birmingham for knee surgery. Four days later I attended the Lincoln-Reagan dinner in Panama City on crutches. Dianne ran up to me gleefully, as if we were the best of friends. The first words out of her mouth were: "Are you getting out of the race *now*?" When I said no, she told me about another candidate in this race who had already withdrawn because of his knee surgery—as if I hadn't gotten the memo. She seemed very disappointed that I wasn't quitting, and several times that night told me I should reconsider. I was really beginning to think she had a reason for wanting me out of the race.

Eddie Hendry spent most of the time before dinner talking to a white-haired retired couple from Panama City Beach who seemed to be his most faithful supporters. They had worked for Eddie on his last campaign for Congress and helped with sign placement and drove a pickup truck with a large "Eddie Hendry for Congress" placard in the truck bed. They were also avid supporters of the Fair Tax—a tax overhaul proposal that replaces all federal income and payroll-based taxes with a progressive national retail sales tax, a provision to ensure that no American pays federal taxes on spending up to the poverty level, a dollar-for-dollar federal revenue replacement, and through companion legislation, the repeal of the Sixteenth Amendment. The couple always wore white cotton tee shirts saying "Support the Fair Tax." They got their signs out before anyone else, and when asked about that, they liked to say, "Well, we had a head start. We had signs left over from last time!"

Steve was there with the beginnings of an entourage: two women manning a small video camera on a tripod. They positioned themselves in the front row, the camera pointed only at Steve, with their arms folded and slouched down in their chairs, their legs crossed akimbo. The women smiled dismissively as if they were disinterested or perhaps didn't think that camera duty at these functions was really a two-woman job. Their only response to the entire evening was to sigh deeply.

In his opening statement, Steve reached in his coat pocket as he said, "I take three things with me everywhere I go: a copy of the Constitution"—he slapped down a pocket-sized pamphlet—"my Bible"—he laid a green New Testament on the table—"and my hunting license." Something in a plastic sleeve hit the table. The other candidates all turned to look at Steve. No one in the audience responded, and in silence, Steve picked up his "show-and-tell" objects and placed them back in his jacket pocket. I never saw him use that line again during the campaign.

The first question from the audience that evening was about an issue that concerned the local voters: "What is your position on offshore drilling and the pending legislation in the Florida legislature to allow drilling three to ten miles off the coast of the Gulf of Mexico?"

This largely retired military audience was worried about the effect on property values, rental income, commercial fishing, sportfishing, and our billion-dollar bread and butter, tourism. But they were also concerned about the military jobs. The Florida Panhandle is home to five military installations: Eglin Air Force Base, Hulbert Field, Whiting Field, Tyndall Air Force Base, and the Pensacola Naval Air Station. The primary missions of Eglin, Hulbert, and Tyndall involve training that could be curtailed by the encroachment of oil rigs. The air-combat training for F-22A Raptor pilots over this area of the Gulf would be especially affected since the electronic emissions from the oil rigs would interfere with the vital communications between the air-battle managers on the ground and the fighter jets in the air.

Eddie was sitting to my left and answered the offshore drilling question first. I don't know if he had spoken to anybody in the room, or to any of the voters in any of the Gulf counties about this issue, but Eddie gave the same answer he always did: He supported the Republican position: drill anywhere and everywhere.

Dianne said she completely supported offshore drilling and pointed out for anyone who did not know that "drill, baby, drill" was the position of the Republican Party. And since I was opposed to the pending offshore drilling legislation, she engaged in eye-rolling—mostly directed at me—to indicate who the "RINOs" (Republicans In Name Only) were in the group. When that did not seem to be working, she attacked my profession: "Lawwwyyers . . . we have too many of 'em in Washington." (At a later debate, she went so far as to say that lawyers should be disqualified from running for Congress. I asked her, "So, you don't think either of your daughters should run for Congress because they are both aspiring lawyers?" She didn't hesitate to throw them under the bus with me and all the other lawyers: "No. Lawyers should not be allowed to serve in Congress.")

I knew the concerns of those who lived in Walton County, had read and studied the issue, and had attended an Oil and Gas Symposium on this new legislation. "I am against this current legislation," I said. "We currently have a buffer in place of 125 miles from the Florida coastline, and this new legislation would allow oil rigs as close as three miles to our shores. At this particular time, I, like most of you, am most concerned about our economy. We cannot afford to do anything that might have a negative impact on our economy, our jobs, our commercial fishing, or our property values. There is simply not a verifiable system that can protect our water and beaches if there is an oil spill within three to ten miles of our coastline. This is not something we will be voting on in Congress, but I am still opposed to it."

David Scholl said that he agreed with my statement and brought up the probable effect of offshore drilling on the district's military population: "We don't want to do anything that would have us lose the military installations because of offshore drilling. Those are important bases and important jobs to this area." (In the ensuing campaign, his position wavered between pro-drilling and pro–military jobs.)

Steve Southerland looked somber as he began to talk. "I tell you, I am so tired of seeing our children come home dead from Afghanistan and the Middle East. You know, that's the business I'm in, and I see it every day." He looked down and somberly shook his head. His voice began to rise a little. "And I am so tired of sending money overseas to people who are trying to kill us. So, yes, we have to stop supporting the people who hate us. And I am just *sick* about helping people who hate us! And we have to stop giving them the ammunition to kill us. So I am for it, we have to drill wherever we can, and we need to do it for our children. But, you know, not only are we in the funeral business, we are also in the timber business up and down the coast. And like Barbara says, people's jobs are important. 'Cause jobs, fishing, and all is important." He nodded thoughtfully and began to pass the microphone back to David Scholl.

Steve's answer prompted a response from an astute woman in the back of the room who was taking notes. "Well, which is it," she said. "Are you for it or against it?"

"What?" said Steve, clearly defensive and confused. "I answered the question."

"Yes, but I don't know what you said." Her pen was poised over her paper. She looked down at her notes. "You said you're for it but you're against it. The last thing we need in Washington is more politicians saying both things at the same time."

The audience laughed.

Steve acted surprised. His eyes darted about as if he were trying to remember what he had said. "No, I didn't say both things—"

Here the attractive blond woman in her fifties cut him off. "I have it right here. I wrote it down. You said that you are for offshore drilling, that we have to drill everywhere. Then you said you agreed with Barbara, who is against offshore drilling. So my question is, where do *you* stand?"

Steve's face was turning red, and sweat was forming on the top of his head. He seemed angry, but it was also clear he did not understand the problem with his answer. "I said," raising his voice, "as long as it's safe I'm *for* it!"

"Well, sure, but that's not the question, is it?"

Steve's eyes squinted and narrowed into slits as he stared at this woman in disgust. He started pulling at his shirt collar.

"The question is not 'are you for offshore drilling *if it is safe*?' We're all for things when they are safe. When you make a decision as a congressman, you will only vote for or against. You won't be able to vote 'for if it is safe.' You see? So, the question I want an answer to is: How will you vote on offshore drilling? Can you answer *that* question?" The woman was cool and unperturbed, her pen once more poised to write.

Steve tried a takedown approach that might have worked in a barbeque joint with his buddies. "I've given you a straight answer. I suggest you just spend some time thinking about it." He leaned back in his chair, and his eyes came to life as he smiled and nodded at her.

The woman slowly put her pen down, and took off her glasses. Everyone in the room turned to look at her. "Steven, that's your name, right? I've been married three times, and the one thing I absolutely know is when a man is not giving me a straight answer!" The audience broke into wild laughter and applause. The woman smiled and looked directly at Southerland with her arms folded across her chest.

Steve sunk down into his seat, glowering at the woman and looking like an animal determined not to get trapped. He spit out, "Well, I've answered the best I could," and sunk down further into his seat.

"Well, maybe, but I still don't know where you stand." The crowd laughed again, and we moved on to other issues.

We were asked about whether we were in favor of term limits for representatives and senators. I said I favored the bill proposed by South Carolina senator Jim DeMint for an amendment to the Constitution limiting representatives to six years (three terms) and senators to twelve years (two terms). I said I believed this was a great way to cure Washington of the self-interest of career politicians. Dianne agreed with me and noted that she had drafted her own "Contract with the People," which included a number of issues, including her promise to limit her own term to eight years. She kept asking me at various forums in front of the audience to sign her "Contract," but I politely declined.

Eddie, David, and Steve all opposed term limits and gave various reasons. Eddie was opposed to term limits because it might result in "more liberal Democrats in Congress." David and Steve thought it would give bureaucrats too much seniority and power. Steve said that such an amendment would not pass because "any amendment will have to be voted on by the people and I don't think the people will do that."

I reached in my purse for my pocket Constitution because there was always so much discussion about it—usually incorrect. I flipped to Article V. "Well, I'm not sure what Steve means about an amendment being voted on by the people, because according to Article V, any amendment to the Constitution has to be ratified by the legislatures of three-fourths of the states or by a constitutional convention. So, the general public doesn't vote; historically, only state legislators have voted on amendments." Someone from the audience asked, "Well, what about a constitutional convention being called to amend the Constitution?" I answered, "Although it is certainly permitted in Article V as a check-and-balance on power implemented in the Constitution, there has never been one since the original convention."

One former military man asked, "Just for whoever wants to answer this one, How will you get along with the NRCC? How do you think you will work with them as a member of Congress?" I had just returned from my meeting with the NRCC the week before, and I shared everything with the group except Sessions's advice to "call before you do anything stupid." I said I thought that the NRCC's Young Guns Program was extremely effective in recruiting and assisting new conservative politicians and equipping them to run successful races. I said I was involved in and hoped to reach the requirements to participate in the Young Guns Program.

Southerland answered without standing up, his hand encircling the wireless microphone. "Well, somebody called me from the NRCC several months ago. Know what I told them? I said, 'Call me back on election night when I'm the winner and I'll talk to you then.' I am not going to be controlled by the NRCC." He smirked but still seemed unsettled by the questioning of the woman taking notes in the back of the room. When the forum ended, he picked up his brochures and left quickly while the other candidates continued to speak with voters.

Later, of course, Southerland forgot his fear of being controlled by the NRCC and entered the Young Guns Program. I wondered whether Representative Sessions had given Steve his private e-mail and number with the admonition to call "before you do anything stupid." But as the campaign progressed, I guessed that either Sessions did not tell the male candidates the same thing, or if he did, they didn't listen. Either way, it seemed to me like doing something stupid might not really hurt you in this campaign. Heck, it looked like the stupider a candidate is, the better he does.

Although there are many smart, accomplished Republicans, they seldom self-identify as intellectuals for fear of being viewed as elitist. Wouldn't it be wise for any political party to draw on everyone's talents, including the intellectuals? Even though William F. Buckley was a staunch conservative, he was always engaging and unpredictable, sometimes supporting candidates like Joe Lieberman and advocating the legalization of drugs. It was Buckley who said, "You know, I've spent my entire lifetime separating the Right from the kooks." One lifetime is clearly not enough for that job.

When the first-quarter federal election campaign report came out on April 30, Southerland was in first place with $154,659, and I was a distant second with $36,675. No matter how silly, stupid, or nonsensical Southerland acted, it didn't hurt his ability to raise money. And the opposite was equally true: being smart had little bearing on fund-raising. Charlie Ranson, the astute lawyer from Tallahassee, raised a little less than I did in the first quarter and withdrew from the race.

6

The Decision

Article I. Section 4.

The times, places and manner of holding elections, for
senators and representatives, shall be prescribed in each state
by the legislature thereof: But the Congress may at any time
by law make or alter such regulations, except as to the places
of choosing senators.

The Federal Election Commission required a quarterly financial disclosure, but the filing itself was not due for thirty days,
which put the first filing due on April 30. I knew, of course, how
much money I had raised, but not the amounts the other candidates
had accumulated. And another deadline was looming: The last day
to formally declare as a candidate for Congress was also April 30,
2010. By that date, a candidate must file with the Florida Division of
Elections and, if running with an affiliated party, submit a check for
$10,400. I thought I had done a good job of fund-raising so far, but
another issue concerned me.

On April 12 and 13, the Tarrance Group, a nationally respected
Republican strategic research and polling firm, conducted a poll asking three hundred "likely registered voters" in District 2 whom they
might vote for in a race between Allen Boyd and Steve Southerland.
The results were summarized in a memo to the NRCC on April 14,
2010. I was told about this poll in a weekly telephone call with staff

members from the Young Guns Program. They told me that the poll showed Southerland beating Boyd 52 percent to 37 percent. It also indicated that a generic Republican would beat a generic Democrat 48 percent to 35 percent. Boyd was identified as "extremely vulnerable," with 61 percent of the voters stating that it was time for a new person in the office. The memo to the NRCC did not mention any of the other District 2 candidates.

The NRCC staffers did not have an explanation for Southerland being the only Republican candidate mentioned in the poll. It was a small sampling, but the results were what the Republican Party wanted to hear: A Republican could beat Boyd, the Blue Dog Democrat, in a predominantly Democratic district. In fact, the poll said that *any* Republican could beat *any* Democrat in the district. Because Southerland was the only Republican candidate mentioned, the poll gave Steve an advantage over the other Republican candidates. On May 11, the *Panama City News Herald* ran the story with the headline "Republican Poll Shows Southerland Trouncing Boyd."

Since returning from Washington, I had been working with the NRCC Young Guns Program mostly on fund-raising, but also on certain other issues that might help my campaign. I had weekly telephone meetings to discuss where the campaign was in respect to its goals and was given certain advice on campaign-related issues. The program had different levels, dependent on the candidate meeting certain goals; if all the goals were met, the candidate finally achieved the ultimate status of Young Gun. Although I understood that I had reached the level of "On the Radar," I later learned that I had not. As one NRCC staffer put it, I was actually "on the radar to be On the Radar." It was all about the money. I hadn't reached my targeted goal of $150,000, but at the time of the poll, Southerland was not a Young Gun either, although he would later become one.

I was aware that the poll would be leaked to the media, although this had not happened by the time I had to declare as a candidate. The circumstances surrounding the poll made me question the wisdom of continuing to work with the NRCC. I did not want to overreact to what seemed like an NRCC endorsement of Southerland. I had naively expected the NRCC to *not* choose between candidates this early, but I now realized it had only one mission, and that was to get a Republican—any Republican—elected.

Someone in District 2 had printed bumper stickers that said: "Anyone but Boyd," and Republicans were happy to have these on their cars and trucks. Although I disagreed with Representative Boyd on certain critical issues (cap and trade, ObamaCare, and some of his reasoning on the economic bailouts), he was neither unintelligent nor uninformed. On the campaign trail, I said: "If we are serious about the direction of this country, and solving problems, we cannot be satisfied to just elect any Republican. We need to elect the person best equipped for the job. If you believe that 'Any Republican will do' in this upcoming election, then I am not your candidate." Eddie Hendry started using the same statement, and I hoped it might give the message some traction. It did not. It is easy to see now that the antigovernment, anti-establishment movement fueled by the Tea Party meant that only ideologically pure conservatives were wanted, and for that, one is as good as another.

It was now three months into the campaign, and I was becoming more uncomfortable at the public forums—both with the other candidates' answers and limited views of the issues and with the outlandish responses of those in attendance. The audiences were responding wildly, as if they were at a church revival, to slogans ("Take it back," "Not going to take it anymore," "We've had enough") and far less enthusiastically to an honest examination of the facts. Maybe Dianne Berryhill was right that I was not one of the sorority girls of the Republican Party and should quit. Maybe I should run, if at all, as an Independent—several of my supporters thought that might be the right move for me. Was I wasting my time? I had two weeks to decide. I called Alex Castellanos to ask his opinion about running as an Independent.

"Why would you do that?"

"Well, a number of reasons: I didn't raise the money I needed in the first quarter, although I came in second. Then there's the poll the NRCC released, which seems to indicate they are behind Southerland. And I have to be so careful and hesitant when speaking truthfully on the issues—the voters seem to prefer an emotionally based campaign, which I don't think appropriate."

"And how will it help for you to switch to an Independent?"

"I could speak truthfully without all the backlash I'm getting from the right wing of the Republican Party. I honestly think the agenda on the right is as bad as the agenda on the left."

"Well, you can't be elected as an Independent—you don't have the name recognition or the money. I really think it's more about whether you're willing to speak the truth when it's uncomfortable. You're right: one agenda only is bad, no matter the side." Alex spoke quietly but firmly. "We don't need people to quit when the party screws up. We need team players. We need real people to go into the locker room and kick ass, to tell the truth and make us all play better. That's what real leaders do. Get in everybody's face. Shake it up for the good of the team. You can only do that if you don't quit."

The only thing Alex forgot to say was "Win one for the Gipper." But he was right. Despite the financial, physical, and emotional cost of continuing this race, this might be the only chance in my life to make this stand. And I thought that despite the odds, it was important for someone to speak up for a moderate and pragmatic view, even if those words could not be heard over all the emotional rhetoric. I still thought that the majority of Republicans would respond more to a thoughtful moderate voice than to a rabid right-wing screed. I gave myself the same advice I give my junior tournament players when they tell me they are scared to go up against a better player. "Do it afraid," I always say. "It's the only way to get through to the next level. Everybody's afraid. Do it afraid, but do it." So, with warning bells sounding about entering the next level, I officially became a candidate for Congress and filed to be on the ballot in the State of Florida.

Unlike Dianne, I was honestly disappointed that Charlie Ranson had withdrawn from the race. I want us to have the best elected officials, no matter who they might be. I had little taste for the political jockeying that candidates undertake in their quest for victory, such as Dianne Berryhill, who switched her candidate affiliation to run as an Independent, and Charlie Crist, the incumbent Florida governor, who defected from the GOP in 2010 to run as an Independent for the U.S. Senate when it became clear that he could not defeat Tea Party–backed Republican Marco Rubio. It did not work for Crist, and it would not work for Dianne, who, as I was finally figuring out, thought it would be an advantage to be the only woman in the race.

I was surprised to see Dianne's husband at a Leon County Republican function after his wife had made the switch to an Independent. "Hey, Don," I said as I shook his hand, "I didn't expect to see you here. I thought y'all had left the Republican Party." He raised his voice, pulled back his shoulders, and jutted out his chest as he said quite pointedly, "We have never left the Republican Party! You need to remember that!" As would often happen during the campaign, I was taken aback at an emotional response to what I thought was simply a factual observation. Apparently, a candidate can run as an NPA (No Party Affiliation) while maintaining their party affiliation. When I considered becoming an Independent candidate, it meant that I would leave the Republican Party.

Silly me. Wrong about politics once again.

7

The Martin Theatre Debate

Article VI. Section 2. Clause 2.

The Senators and Representatives before mentioned, and the
Members of the several State Legislatures, and all executive
and judicial Officers, both of the United States and of the
several States, shall be bound by Oath or Affirmation, to
support this Constitution; *but no religious Test shall ever be
required as a Qualification to any Office or public Trust under
the United States.* (italics added)

The first major debate for the Republican primary candidates
was at the Martin Theatre in Panama City on May 18. The Republican primary field now consisted of Southerland, Hendry,
Scholl, newcomer Ron McNeil, and me. Before the debate there was
time to meet citizens in the lobby. The candidates worked the room,
handing out campaign literature and answering questions from the
voters. Southerland's people handed out "Have you had enough?"
stickers to people as they entered the theater.

We were all summoned backstage before the debate to pull numbers for location on the stage and for who would give the first opening statement. My opponents allowed me to go first as the only
woman, and I selected "No. 1."

While we were still backstage, Greg Marr of the Big Bend Republican Club told me the date of the Woman's Club of Tallahassee

debate had been changed to accommodate one of the candidates. I told him I would check my calendar and let him know if I was available on the new date. He said abruptly, "Well, that's the date and we're not changing it again. If you can't make it, there will be an empty chair." I said, "So, you will accommodate one candidate but not all the candidates?" He said, "That's the date. That's the way it is," and then turned and walked offstage into the audience. Eddie Hendry was standing near me and said, "Barbara, I'm sorry. I'm the reason they changed the date because I had a work issue. I think I should miss it if anyone has to." I said, "Eddie, that's fine. I don't know if I have a problem with it. I just thought they would want to accommodate everyone, and that surprises me a little."

I had never felt any discrimination practicing law, even though being a trial lawyer has historically been the province of men. Before I entered law school, my father and I discussed the type of law I might practice. Growing up in a courtroom since I was about seven years old, I was both comfortable and interested in a litigation practice. But I knew it was not the usual choice for women attorneys. I asked my father if he knew any women lawyers who were good in the courtroom. I will always cherish his response: "No, honey, I don't. But that doesn't mean there aren't any, and more importantly, that doesn't mean you can't be a good one. It's all a matter of whether you're suited for it." Those words assumed even more importance to me as my father died during the second week of my first year in law school. I had chosen Cumberland Law School in Birmingham, Alabama, because my father was a 1938 graduate of Cumberland when it was located in Lebanon, Tennessee, and because it had an outstanding trial advocacy program. I was involved and successful in the trial program, winning numerous competitions, serving on the Trial Advocacy Board my senior year, and becoming the first woman to be a member of the ABA trial team in 1984. That year Cumberland won both the regional and national competitions.

So while I was used to competing with men in the legal profession, I was not accustomed to discriminatory statements or actions related to my gender. But I was beginning to experience disparate treatment on the campaign trail. In early March, the president of the South Walton County Republican Club, Robert Sullivan, had told me, "You might want to reconsider being in the race. Steve has this thing pretty well sewn up." Surprised that a party leader would make such a statement, I said, "So, you think I should just drop out, then?" "Wouldn't be a bad idea," Sullivan replied. And Panama City conservative talk-show host Burnie Thompson would not return my phone calls or e-mails asking to be on his show. He even ignored a letter requesting equal air time, as mandated by the Federal Communications Commission. He finally put me on the show when I reached him by cell phone and said, "Burnie, I think I can get elected to Congress easier than I can get on your show." He was cordial enough on the air, and was impressed by my knowledge of the Constitution. Something was clearly amiss, but I did not know if the overt discrimination was because of my gender or my lack of right-wing fanaticism.

The Martin Theatre Debate was sold out and local conservative talk-show host Doc Washburn, whom I had come to know and respect for his fairness, was the moderator. In my opening statement, I stuck to my plan, focusing on the economy and national security. I addressed the constitutional issues that were eroding our freedoms and said that the Framers of the Constitution placed limitations on government to ensure individual freedom. I commented on the lack of authority of Congress to enact the current health-care bill, and said that I believed such "political pandering would backfire." I discussed the federal authority to make laws regarding immigration and that we needed to enforce those provisions that had been in the 1986 Simpson-Mazzoli Bill, which gave amnesty to illegal immigrants and promised to secure the border and enforce employer verification. I received applause when I said that English should be the official language.

The serious discussion on the issues that I was anticipating, and for which I had prepared, did not happen. Instead, every answer by my opponents was supersaturated with love of family, God, and country. We seemed to be participating in a contest for the best American, the best family, or the most religious. Scholl's military service seemed to win him the label "most patriotic"; Southerland took the prize for "best extended family"; Hendry won "most anti-Obama"; and "best Christian" was a draw. Southerland talked about

The first public debate of the campaign at the Martin Theatre in Panama City on May 18, 2010. *Left to right:* me, Scholl, Hendry, McNeil, and Southerland. I thought I was doing a good job, but the other candidates seem to look at me as if I didn't get it. They were right, and I was wrong.

how his grandfather had brought him to the Martin Theatre to see his first movie, the number of members in his family, and walking the streets of Panama City as a child. Scholl discussed "marching with Reagan" at his inauguration, his military service as a pilot, and his mother's recent struggle with cancer and how that related to his pro-life views on abortion. He said President Obama was "stealing from our children, socializing medicine, and the change he wants is to change us." Hendry talked about his pro-life views as well as how that related to one of his children, growing up in Taylor County, attending the Citadel, and being prepared to "take on Obama." Hendry claimed, "Obama is our biggest threat to national security." But the new guy, Ron McNeil, stole the show and walked away with "most entertaining."

Ron McNeil made his first campaign appearance at this forum. He is a tall, good-looking man in his mid-sixties without even a speck of gray in his hair. He grew up on a farm and had become a successful inventor. He spoke with a real southern drawl and mumbled so that it was hard to understand him. Ron is a real character, and he loved to make the audience laugh. I don't think he was trying to be funny; he just doesn't filter anything he says—which can be refreshing. He is a real rugged kind of guy you would be glad to see if your tractor was stuck in the mud on the farm, or you had a bear chasing you through the back woods.

But Ron's political views don't seem to have evolved beyond 1964. Political correctness was something somebody came up with just to annoy Ron, and he didn't mind telling you that. One statement that got a huge laugh was when he was asked about his stand on the military policy of "Don't ask, don't tell." Ron weaved a little behind the podium before he drawled, "Well, them folks ain't voting for me anyway, so I don't think it matters what I think." Southerland, who was standing next to Ron, laughed so hard I thought he might have to leave the stage—he was doubled over and slapping Ron on the back. When asked what he thought about illegal immigration, Ron said the illegal immigrants were "running over the border like rabbits" and they needed to be "bused back to Mexico." The remark made me cringe, but no one else seemed bothered by it. Once again Steve was laughing so hard he was losing his breath. Ron got another big laugh when he said he would do away with the Internal Revenue Service. He said he had fought the IRS before and he would be "glad to get rid of them." I thought it might be poor form in a run for Congress to admit that you had been in litigation with the IRS, but it did not bother Ron one bit. He warned IRS employees not to vote for him because if he won, they would be out of a job. The audience laughed and applauded. The experience felt more like being in a college locker room than a congressional race.

David Scholl and Ron McNeil found a way to bring President Reagan into every answer. David had marched in Reagan's inaugural parade. Ron had his picture taken with President Reagan when Ron ran for Congress in 1984. Ron lost that race, but he was proud of being voted the "most conservative candidate for Congress." Ron also had another picture he liked to show voters—Ron as a young man on his horse "Duke," wearing a Stetson, a goatee, and looking all cowboy. Ron said that night, and at every event thereafter: "I am a cross between John Wayne and Ronald Reagan." I understood why he wanted to be identified with Reagan, but it took a while to un-

> One could only ask, "What would Ronald Reagan do about the political shenanigans that are going on in Washington?"

Ronald Reagan and Ron McNeil, meeting at the White House during Reagan's Presidency and McNeil's run for US Congress. McNeil was voted the top non-incumbent candidate for US Congress in the nation by Lee Atwater and the National Republican Party at that time.

Bold & Determined Leadership	A True Constitutional Conservative
Promotion of Limited Government	Proponent for Free Enterprise
Vision for Preserving America's Future	Advocate for Lower & Fair Taxation

Ron McNeil for U.S. Congress

Flier for candidate Ron McNeil. The photograph of him with President Ronald Reagan is from McNeil's prior congressional run in 1982. McNeil liked to say he was "a cross between Ron Reagan and John Wayne." He did look a little like both of them, but I don't think that's what he meant.

derstand the reference to John Wayne. Then I remembered a media flap over Wayne's outspoken and politically incorrect statements: In a 1971 *Playboy* interview, Wayne had infamously offended Native Americans (we stole the land because we needed it, and we don't owe them anything) and blacks ("I believe in white supremacy") and denigrated welfare ("need to stop giving money to people sitting on their backsides and complaining"). But I doubt anyone in the audience remembered the Duke's political views, so maybe Ron was just trying to identify with a real outspoken "don't tell me what to do" cowboy. They mostly found Ron entertaining, and more than one person said Ron needed his own talk show.

I was surprised that the focus at this first public debate was on matters completely unrelated to the current events, the nation's problems, or any possible solutions to those problems. The candidates talked about the size of their families and how long they had lived in a certain county and who their relatives were. They talked about how much they loved their country: Looking defiantly at the other candidates who lacked military service, which was all of us, Scholl said, "I didn't just stumble on my patriotism." Besides Reagan, the Founding Fathers were often invoked: Southerland particularly liked Ben Franklin, and would later mention Madison, Jefferson, and Hamilton. Eddie favored Thomas Jefferson and liked to refer to himself as a "Federalist"—even though Jefferson was anti-Federalist.

They brought God into the conversation as much as possible: They liked to call themselves "Christian men" and talked about where they went to church and Sunday school. They never suggested we should "love our enemies" or pray for those in authority. Instead, they called President Obama "evil" and said aggressive things like they "would go Old Testament on anybody who messed with their family." Besides Obama and his administration, they generally all made derogatory comments about then-governor Charlie Crist, Mexicans, Muslims, and gays. Everyone in this race was a Christian, but the men really liked to lay it on thick: They would not answer a straightforward question on policy if they had an opportunity to preach. When asked, for example, about overturning *Roe v. Wade*, all the men took all their allotted time to do more than answer the question, discussing as well the immorality of abortion, and personal family issues that they related to the sanctity of life and the religious aspects of life and death. When the moderator, Doc Washburn, asked me, "Ms. Olschner, would you like to see *Roe v. Wade* overturned?" I answered, "Yes." We continued looking at each other for a beat or three before he nodded his head toward me and gave me a slight eye bob. I said,

"Well, the question is 'Would I like to see *Roe v. Wade* overturned?' My answer is 'Yes.'" The audience laughed and began to applaud, and later this was mentioned as an example of my pragmatism. My opinion was based more on the strained legal reasoning in *Roe v. Wade*, but no one ever asked, or seemed to care, about my rationale. All these issues have complexities that require a sincere struggle to reach the correct result. Criminalization of abortion is not the appropriate remedy. The life of the unborn deserves protection as does the health and well-being of the mother. As a Baptist preacher said to me, "I am certainly pro-life; but I struggle with denying abortions when there has been rape or incest." My thought is that *Roe v. Wade* is not the best way to handle these issues, not that I think it should be more stringent or we should return to criminal punishment for abortions. This was also not an issue I thought we should be focused on with our economy in such shambles.

The next week on Doc's radio show, I elaborated: "We have got to stop wasting so much time and focus on the important issues. That is how I would work in Congress. I think the economy and the national debt are the biggest issues we face, and we must focus our time, energy, and talents on resolving those issues first. As to any other issues, let's answer the question, whatever it is, and move on." I continually said that this was a two-year job and that for twenty-four months we needed to focus first and foremost on our economy. Although people seemed to agree, they really wanted to know, first and foremost, whether you passed their ideological litmus test.

The vilification of President Obama received the most applause. The headline in the next day's *Panama City News Herald* was "Candidates Bond in Disgust over Obama." That was, however, not my position, and it bothered me to be tagged with that line. I disagreed with many of Obama's policies, but I repeatedly said in the debate that you cannot solve problems by calling people names or attacking their character—expressing anger is not a professional way to resolve disagreements. I also said that as a tennis player I had been taught the Greek proverb "Whom the gods wish to destroy, they first make mad." Later, I was criticized by one of my conservative supporters for using this quote in the debate. "That's a good way for people to think you are not a Christian," she said. "Because I quoted

Ancient literature?" I asked. "No, because you suggested there are gods rather than one God. Don't do that again if you want to win." The petty and juvenile snipes of my opponents, as well as some of my supporters, embarrassed and concerned me. How could we possibly elect competent leaders with such attitudes? I was continually surprised by the audience's obvious encouragement of extreme statements that could only be described as "tribal politics."

The issue of religion came up frequently, not only that night, but as the campaign dragged on, and the discussion reached a fevered pitch with the news that Muslims were building a mosque near Ground Zero. McNeil was out in front on that issue, trumpeting that "Muslims were out to destroy our way of living." He said he wanted the mosque built "nine floors underground so that as a Christian man, he could walk on it." Ron said it was fine with him to "just blow the mosque up." He said it was "our job as Christians to stand up against the Muslims." Scholl said he would "do everything in his power to fight against the building of that mosque."

Generally, I would read the portion of the First Amendment that stated: "Congress shall make no law respecting an establishment of religion, or prohibiting the free exercise thereof. . . ." I would remind them that, like it or not, the Muslims had the constitutional right to build the mosque wherever they wanted. But that didn't alter the other candidates' expressions of anger about or determination to fight the mosque, and it didn't alter the applause such declarations received from the audience. I was mystified by the outcry over protecting the Constitution from citizens who, quite frankly, lacked knowledge or understanding of the document itself. Was this, I asked myself, only a rallying rhetorical cry meant to incite people to come to the polls to vote? How can you possibly "defend your Constitution" when you don't have any idea what it says?

All my opponents that night talked about being mad and how they were "not going to take it anymore." I wondered if that worried anyone except me. I also wondered whether the audience was applauding and laughing *at* the men's outlandish statements or because they agreed *with* the outlandish statements. They applauded my statement that I would sign on to the repeal of the health-care bill, but that was expected. And when I was asked whether we should repeal the "Don't ask, don't tell" policy, I responded by saying we should follow our military advisors on that issue. But I pressed my pragmatic side to the forefront when I said: "Look, if we don't focus on our economy and get a handle on our national debt, we are not going to have anything to ask or anybody to tell." When the audience broke out into wild applause, I took that as an expression of voters' interest in the serious issues, but, on reflection, I think they were just enjoying the evening's entertainment and applauding the verbal pyrotechnics that spiced it up. That night I referred to the four men onstage with me as my "gentleman opponents." But after that debate, in which they launched their vitriolic attacks not only against me, but against anyone who disagreed with their views, I would not be tempted to call them that again.

8

The Tea Party Festival

Fourteenth Amendment. Section 3. (1868)

No person shall be a Senator or Representative in Congress,
or elector of President and Vice-President, or hold any
office, civil or military, under the United States, or under any
State, who, having previously taken an oath, as a member of
Congress, or as an officer of the United States, or as a member
of any State legislature, or as an executive or judicial officer
of any State, to support the Constitution of the United States,
shall have engaged in insurrection or rebellion against the
same, or given aid or comfort to the enemies thereof.

In the 2010 election, the Tea Party was a relatively new movement, having originated with an irate television news reporter in
Chicago in 2009 and grown to a grassroots organization driven
by the ideological elite with billionaire support. But when I began
my campaign, I thought it was just a grassroots organization of vo-
cal and concerned citizens. Their most cited issues of less government, less taxation, the national debt, and the deficit seemed valid
concerns, although their articulation of those concerns was often
one-dimensional. The slogan "Take our country back" seemed too
vague—what did that really mean? Take it back from the liberals
who had only been in power since 2009? Take it back from the last
eight years of Republican administrations that had increased spending and the debt?

Unlike the other candidates, I did not court this group's vote, so I was surprised when Walton County's Tea Party group endorsed me. (I was told this endorsement had created friction in the group as I was not "one of them," but they recognized that I was knowledgeable about the Constitution.) I did not attend any Tea Party meetings. But when I was invited to the Tea Party Festival in the far eastern part of the district, I thought I should attend.

Perry is a tiny town of fewer than seven thousand souls in the southeastern corner of the Second Congressional District. The average household income is a third less than Florida's median. There is little diversity here—just white people and black people for generations. Many of the candidates for federal and state offices had set up tents and staff at the fairground just outside Perry for this Tea Party outdoor food and music festival. It was a hot, humid day in late May 2010 as I greeted folks and talked politics. Local country bands and singers performed on the outdoor stage, food vendors hawked hot dogs, ice cream, and lemonade, and fund-raisers raffled American-eagle quilts and U.S. flags.

My campaign table with signs and campaign materials was positioned next to that of one of the candidates for governor, Bill McCollum, along the path to the air-conditioned building that housed, among other things, the restrooms—a prime location. Several of the young men from McCollum's staff had become friends, so we chatted with each other and with the voters milling around, picking up campaign material and talking about the issues.

I am a southerner and, as we say, born and bred in the South. My mother's family is from eastern North Carolina, and my father's family moved to North Carolina from New Orleans. I have never lived outside of the South, and I understand the cultural nuances of this region. This allows me to say what any historian will confess is true: the South is, and has always been, distinctive. As a southerner, I feel free to say that the South is nothing short of peculiar. We are territorial over things that are not ours, combative when we have the short end of the stick, stubborn to a fault—although we see this as a virtue—clannish in our culture, and hold grudges for generations. A circuit court judge in north Alabama once refused to plant the prize-winning Mr. Lincoln in his rose garden. His reasoning: "I'm not about to have that damn Mr. Lincoln on my property!" The year: 1969, more than a hundred years since the Civil War had ended.

The young man who walked up to me at a Tea Party Festival in Perry, Florida, was clearly a southerner. Dressed in desert camouflage shorts and green tee shirt, his lower lip bulged with a plug of tobacco; a brown roil of juice nestled in the corner of his mouth. His eyes were small, round, and dark. His hair was buzzed a little too close, and he had neglected to shave for days. He might have spent the last several days in a fish camp, or he could have been down on his luck. He did, however, stand out from the rest of the folks at this Tea Party event, who were dressed mostly in neat cotton pants, skirts, jeans, and plaid short-sleeved shirts appropriate for the hot weather. He was also at least forty years younger than the average person in attendance that day.

During a pause in the activity of people milling around, the young man approached me in a sideways manner. He looked down at his untied, worn work boots and shouted out to me, "Hey, I have a question."

I introduced myself, "Hello. I'm Barbara Olschner and I'm running for Congress." I extended my hand.

"Yeah. I know who you are." He gave a laugh masquerading as a snort as he jerked his head toward my campaign signs. "That's why I came over here—to talk to you." He continued to laugh derisively to himself while ignoring my outstretched hand. He was clearly uncomfortable. His expression and mannerisms put me on guard. As he continued chuckling to himself, I was reminded of a game greatly enjoyed in the South: make the city slicker look stupid and display the underdog's superior wit.

At the check-out counter of a southern convenience store, you may see a group of men sitting around a table in the back drinking coffee or Cokes, some with toothpicks wedged into the corners of their mouths. If you notice that they are looking at you in an odd way, rolling their eyes and nodding their heads in a conspiratorial fashion while quietly snickering, you can be sure the game is on. My best advice: If you're not a member of the team, you can't play this game. Protect yourself. Move on.

Anyone who has watched Bugs Bunny or Roadrunner cartoons

recognizes the theme of this game: the underdog uses his wits to survive. In the South, some folks still think of themselves as underdogs because of our history of having fought the Yankees and having been occupied by federal troops after we lost. And long before Bugs Bunny and the Roadrunner, most southerners were familiar with the underdog theme through the tales of Uncle Remus—particularly the one in which Brer Rabbit pleads with Brer Fox *not* to throw him in the briar patch. Which, of course, Brer Fox does. "I was bred and born in the briar patch, Brer Fox," the rabbit calls derisively while hopping away. "Bred and born in the briar patch." The name of this game is "Who's the Dumb Ass Now?"

I myself have been an unwilling participant on occasions. You don't have to be a Yankee—any outsider will do—but you do have to be in some way a threat to "the way things are done." Outsmarting a "smarty pants" provides the unending delight of the game. Some of the South-will-rise-again rhetoric is probably based on the notion that we just haven't quite figured out how to make the North the dumb ass, given that they beat us. It's one of the reasons that we can't keep from being derisive about a Yankee and pointing out his lack of manners, his peculiar dress and speech, his lack of social graces. We know in our hearts, after 150 years, that this is not enough to win the game, but we can't stop.

Once I witnessed a very sophisticated and attractive Italian man try to buy dog food in a ramshackle, rundown grocery store and one-pump gas station in lower Alabama. His fine-tailored Merino wool suit was all trimly buttoned as he tried to find a place to put the soles of his exquisite cognac leather shoes where they would not stick to the unlevel floor. He was in the doorway gesturing with his thumb pressed up against his forefingers as he said, "Dog-a food-a."

The obviously related men behind the counter were chewing on broom straws and sucking their teeth as they said, "Whatcha say there Frenchy? Turpentine-a? Gasoline-a?"

I don't know how long this charade had been going on, but as I walked around the Italian man I said to the brothers, "Could you just get the man some dog food?" "Aww, jeez, shucks. We didn't get that," the brothers said as they elbowed each other with laughter while pointing to a bag of Purina on the shelf. With a delicate and handsome gesture, the gentleman bowed toward me as he said, "Grazie." I replied, "Prego. Welcome to Alabama."

Although I have been around this game all my life, I don't like it. It can be humorous, but the game also has a more sinister side. I didn't know which way this was going with the man in the green shirt, but his laughter seemed to indicate that he needed the upper hand. I decided to proceed cautiously. I asked him, "And what is your name?"

"Uh," and he uttered something unintelligible like "Pfffen" while spitting brown tobacco juice near his boots. He looked up and gave me a smug smile. He appeared pleased to have not told me his name as he snorted in laughter again. He moved his nose and mouth together as his bottom lip stuck out and he said, "Now, my question for you. Yep. Something I need to know 'fore I vote fer you."

Pfffen was trying to find a comfortable stance while moving his tobacco around inside his cheek and wiping sweat from his brow. He picked at his tee shirt and dog tags, and I wondered how long it would take in this heat and humidity to get to his question. "'Cause I got to know this, 'cause I could, you know, vote fer you." He seemed to relish taking this time to make his demands known.

After a pause, he finally spoke. "I need to know this. I want a congressman or WOMAN"—this last word said slowly and in a highly exaggerated tone—"who, when they go to Congress, will plant their feet and not move. Right or wrong. Once they plant their feet, whether they are right or wrong, I want someone who will not move. That's what I'm looking fer. Someone who will stay with his or her feet planted. That chu?" He spread his feet and crossed his arms on his chest and only now looked directly at me with an intense stare.

"No," I said. "That's not me. If I am wrong in my position, wrong in my understanding, I will change my stand."

"Nope," he said, "WRONG ANSWER! I want someone who WILL NOT BUDGE!!!"

This angry tone when my opinion differed from someone else's was by now becoming all too familiar. But this young man, by his appearance and demeanor, was a little threatening. Like most women in the South, I have been taught to watch out for these guys—they can be rough but harmless, or mean and dangerous. It would have been so simple to say, "That's right, son. I'm not moving. You can count on me!" and collect his vote while laughing all the way to the finish line, thinking, "What a dumb ass!" But I did not do that.

"Well, I disagree. It's the right answer because I've told you the truth. I think that is important to hear the truth from people who are running for office. If I have a stand on an issue, but I learn something that convinces me that my stand is wrong, it's more important to me that we make the best decisions for this country. And that might mean admitting I'm wrong and changing my stand. That's what I'll do." I nodded politely toward him. "But it's up to you to vote the way you think is right."

His eyes told me that he thought this was a trick answer, but he could not find the trick. "Well, we didn't back off to the Yankees, and they were beatin' the stew outta us."

I thought to myself, "Are you kidding me?" But instead, I said, "I'm from the South, just like you, but the South surrendered because we lost." I nodded gently. "That war is done and over with."

"Not to me it ain't," he said.

"Well, it was nearly 150 years ago; we tried the states' rights issue of 'don't tell us what to do' and lost. More than six hundred thousand Americans died in that war."

"Well," he said, "we shoulda never backed down from that fight, and that's what I want in my CongressMAN"—with emphasis on the last syllable. He stood with his arms crossed and stomped his left foot like a child having a tantrum. His abrupt motion jangled the dog tags around his neck. I could not imagine that this young man had served in the military, and so I said, "What branch of the military did you serve in?" He blew air out of his cheeks in disgust as he said, "Poofffff—None!"

I said nothing more because it was now fairly clear to me what we were really talking about. It was not just the idea that "the South will rise again" and have another go at it. This young man represented a large segment of the electorate who view issues only on the visceral level of how they want things to be in *their* America. He was looking for someone who would give him "his America," no matter the cost.

"I understand what you're saying," I said. "I've given you my answer. You need to do what you think is best."

"What the hell is that supposed to mean? And who the hell are you to tell somebody what to do?" He turned angrily on his worn heels, gave another derisive snort, and walked off muttering something under his breath.

With country music in the background and the aroma of hot dogs and onions in the air, I was not really afraid of this young man. But something in Pfffen's manner bothered me. I have been exposed to dangerous men—criminals, rapists, and murderers. I tagged along with my father to the jailhouse when he would visit his clients, and in my own law practice, I've been inside prisons, mostly deposing inmates about their prior lives. These experiences have taught me to know that a sense of danger causes heightened awareness.

To stifle this feeling, I talked with some of my campaign staff and volunteers who were making their way back from the ice-cream and funnel-cake concessions. They all had the same comment, "Just a redneck. A small segment of the voting public. Forget about it." But I kept thinking about my conversation with him. Was he capable of anything more than petulant behavior? I don't know what happens to a person's soul, what things get dropped into the mix that can never be retrieved.

I remembered a childhood incident that had shaped my decisions about life—a seventh-grade field trip to Central Prison in Raleigh, North Carolina. For some reason, we were not taken to see an art or natural history museum, the state legislature, or the Governor's Mansion—any of the places one would expect the educated children of the local gentry to inhabit one day.

Our teacher, bless her heart, had a problem showing up on time for class, generally missing the first hour or so. She also had difficulty matching her clothing, and there was the little problem of confining lipstick to her lips. Some of the children who knew more about the consumption and effects of spirits said she had a drinking problem.

As we wandered through the first and largest prison in North Carolina, Miss Bless Her Heart said we were in for a special treat. We rounded a corner and saw an enclosed room with glass panels for viewing. With lipstick applied in reckless abandon, our teacher pointed with her purse-draped arm and shouted, "Look! It's Old Yella."

Nope, not the Disney *Old Yeller* tear-jerker dog movie, which we would have liked, but a pair of chairs designed for the sole purpose of killing folks. I remember standing there in absolute horror as our teacher also said, with a strange hint of pride, that there had been a mother-daughter joint electrocution in 1955, the last time a woman was put to death in North Carolina, and added that "there hasn't been a joint execution since."

Neither I, nor any of my lily-white, blue-eyed classmates, were on a path to a life of crime. But staring at those grotesque matching yellow chairs I vowed to myself, "Whatever it takes, whatever I have to do or not do, I will never end up in that room, in one of those chairs!"

Thanks to the Web, unavailable in 1964, I know that much of what Miss Bless Her Heart said was not true. At that time in North Carolina, execution was by gas, not electrocution. There was no chair in North Carolina named "Old Yella." And there were no double executions ever in North Carolina. Maybe she just had a really grizzly imagination that she put to good use steering seventh-graders away from a life of crime. But we were already separated by social class from the majority of those who find themselves behind bars. People of color, with low levels of education, family instability, and lack of financial resources dominate in prison populations.

Pfffen reminded me just how truly separated we are in our society, and of the frustration and desperation that comes from seeing yourself at risk for a change you neither want nor think will include you. And so many in the South, and other places as well, use this arrogant, domineering tone to attempt to bully others.

And here is what Pfffen and many other southern boys don't get: Dixie lost, but America won. Had the South won the "War of Northern Aggression," the United States could never have become the champion of democracy and freedom around the globe. We would have become more like Europe, a collection of small countries rather than a powerful singular nation of people with shared principles and ideals. And the great things America has accomplished as a beacon of freedom and democracy simply would not have existed.

But Pfffen's rage and anger had to be over more than our disagreement. It was that he needed certainty, not only that his ideology was correct, but also that someone in authority would help him hold on to it against the influx of others determined to displace him. I was beginning to understand what we are up against as a nation in trying to come together for the greater good. It is not just that they want you to be like them; they need assurance that you are them, and therefore they won't become—or remain—outsiders. These voters need their candidates and elected officials to be a political and social mirror reflecting themselves in looks, values, beliefs, and prejudices. If that is true, I thought to myself, how do we ever bridge the gap between these different groups?

At the end of the day, as I was getting ready to leave, Pfffen reappeared. My volunteers had left and my staff had gone to the car to load up campaign paraphernalia. I was alone as he sidled up to me.

"Hey! I've been looking fer you. And, uh, I've been thinking of what you said." Well, this didn't sound good. I waited.

"Yep," he said with a toothy grin and a slight edge to his voice as he stepped a little too close to me, "I decided that I'll make a deal with you. If you win, I'll pray for you. You understand what I'm saying?" He smiled and his eyes narrowed as he slowly leaned toward me. It was the aggressive movement of a bully.

"I think so," I said quietly. "You think folks better be praying for my safety if I win."

"Yep," he said, now grinning from big ear to big ear, his Adam's apple bobbing up and down. Like my southern female relatives, some well into their nineties, I don't really "cotton" to someone trying to scare me, much less make me run like a bunny. This time I was willing to plant my feet and not move.

"Well, are you a Christian?" I said calmly.

"Yep, that I am," he said.

"Well, don't you think you should pray for God's will to be done?"

"Yeah, right! But I'm only going to be praying *if* you win. That's my deal! 'Cause yore going to need it." He said this with a singsong rhythm.

I sincerely wanted to reach this young man, not for his vote, but because of what divides us. But I did not know how to do that. I knew he had sought me out at the end of the day to feel like he had won, and I understood his oblique threats. But I also knew that anything I said would be lost on him. He did not speak the language of compromise, and I did not speak the language of intolerance. I really saw, for the first time, the impossibility of bringing people together who lack the capacity, intellectually, emotionally, or socially, to compromise.

My response to him was weak, but I was greatly demoralized as I said to him, "If you are truly a praying man, then this country needs your prayers now, more than ever. Not just for me, but we need to be able to get along and solve our problems. We don't need another Civil War."

Pfffen smiled, pleased that he had won. His index finger pointed from his temple to me as he said, "Nup, that's my deal. Only goin' to pray IF you win." And with a swagger in his gait, he walked away.

My staff was wrong: it was too simplistic to call Pfffen an "uneducated redneck" who represents a small segment of the population. This was an attitude that demanded lack of compromise, intolerance for differing opinions, and an absolute dogma of "my way or the highway." This attitude, sadly, wasn't confined to a rural, uneducated, southern segment of the Republican population. This attitude was also found in navy-blue suits and expensive dress shoes and came packaged by those with billions of dollars to drive their agenda home. But the question that remained for me, and to which I did not know the answer, was this: Is this attitude only a small segment of an undereducated rural population in the Panhandle or the controlling faction of the Republican Party?

As I walked to my car, I overheard two older gentlemen talking to each other. One man said, "Do you know the best way to talk to a liberal?" The other fellow looked down at the ground and shook his head, saying, "No, sir, I sure don't." "Well, when we have a conservative Congress and a conservative president, then you don't have to even try." Both men laughed, slapping each other on the back.

As I began my four-hour drive back to Walton County, I thought, if we reject those candidates with the skills to build consensus across the party lines, then we remain in gridlock unable to remedy any of the problems we face. If we are unable to solve the mounting problems facing us, then what will eventually happen to this great America?

You can win the battle and wind up with candidates who will not compromise, but lose the war for the success of America.

And when that happens, who's the dumb ass now?

9

The Dowling Park Debate

Article VI. Clause 2.

This Constitution, and the Laws of the United States which shall be made in Pursuance thereof . . . , shall be the supreme Law of the Land; and the Judges in every State shall be bound thereby; any Thing in the Constitution or Laws of any State to the Contrary notwithstanding.

The Dowling Park Debate was set in the middle of absolute nowhere. The Florida heat and humidity had buckled the county two-lane asphalt road leading to the Advent Christian Village Conference & Retreat Center—a two-hour drive southeast from Tallahassee past stark and lonely clumps of sandy scrub pines into Suwannee County. Because there was little cell-phone coverage, it was eerily quiet once I left Interstate 10.

The Advent Christian Village at Dowling Park, Florida, is the oldest retirement village in the state. Founded in 1913 on 1,200 wooded acres overlooking the Suwannee River, the Village is still very active, and that night residents had organized a forum and reception for the Republican candidates. If they chose to, the candidates could spend the night in the conference center, but I had an early radio show the next day in Tallahassee, and since the forum started at 4:30 p.m., I would have plenty of time to drive back and stay at the Hotel Duval in Tallahassee, where I knew I could get a great cup of Starbucks coffee early the next morning.

A little before 4:00 p.m. I approached the conference center, where two men in their seventies wearing baseball hats, short-sleeved shirts, and orange reflective safety vests waved at me to drive into the parking circle. The red, white, and blue magnetic campaign signs announcing my candidacy were on both sides of my car.

I stopped the car and rolled down the window and felt the cool cabin air escape as both men bent their lanky frames at the waist to peer in and give their best newcomer smile. With both faces filling the window frame and their heads almost touching, they sucked in the cool air as one said, "Hey there."

"Hello," I said, "I'm Barbara Olschner." I raised my shoulders a little and leaned toward the passenger seat as they moved in further. They kept their smiles and nodded.

"We're having the candidates for Congress speaking tonight. Are you here to listen to them?" said the taller of the two gentlemen, excitement in his voice.

"Well, I *am* one of the candidates for Congress. I'm Barbara," and with my index finger I pointed down to the red, white, and blue magnetic campaign sign on the door. They backed up in tandem and looked at it. The taller fellow looked a little perplexed and turned his head to look at the shorter one, who said, "That's right, Bob, I think there is a lady candidate, remember? She might be running for Congress, too. She could be right." They both nodded at each other and turned again to smile.

"I guess it could be," Bob said, as he nodded his head at his friend and then at me. Not wanting to argue with them about my existence, I just smiled and found myself bobbing my head in rhythm with them. Bob placed his hand on the car and said, "You gonna want to eat supper?"

"No, I don't think so, but thank you," I said as the bright sun reflected a searing glare off the white hood of my car.

"Well, supper is going on right now if you want," said Bob, and his friend chimed in, "You might have to hurry." Bob added. "You just go right in that building there." And with arthritic necks they both turned their entire bodies to point to the covered walkway to their left.

"Thank you," I said, but I didn't think they heard me. When they turned back again, I said, "Thank you," and they both seemed a little unsure about why I was thanking them.

Bob said, "Park anywhere," and they both moved again in unison, as their pale white arms flapped like large cranes as they pointed around the circle. If I could park anywhere, I wondered why Bob and his friend were there. I circled around, went back on the street, and parked.

Just as Bob said, supper was still going on when I walked into the center. Sunlight streamed through large, spotless windows. The residents were dressed casually in striped or plaid short-sleeved shirts, light-blue denim, and assorted knit pants and tops. I noticed some local politicians from Suwannee County, including Carl Meese, who was the chairman of the local Republican Party and had been a candidate for Congressional District 2 before he had withdrawn. Tea Party favorite Kris Anne Hall was there also with her husband and young son. A former assistant state attorney, she allegedly had been fired for teaching the Constitution to Tea Party groups. I did not know the entire story, but she was certainly a popular figure.

I walked into the reception area where soft drinks, coffee, and cookies were available and appraised the crowd—a good mixture of folks from the South and Midwest and a few retired military folks as well. Miss Charlotte, one of the retired members of the Village, was my guide for the evening. She was very kind, gracious, and tall, with a perpetual smile. Her knit pants hung over sturdy and sensible shoes. As she walked over to meet me and leaned down to hug me, I smelled lemon and Baby Magic. She probably made a terrific lemon Bundt cake and might have just finished baking one. As she hugged me, she said, "I am so, so delighted, delighted to meet you." She stood up and held my hand as she said with a somewhat conspiratorial tone and midwestern twang, "Don't you just love our Sarah?" Miss Charlotte scrunched up her shoulders as she waited for my reply.

Sometimes it was hard to keep up with the non sequiturs at the Village, but I knew we were talking about former Alaska governor and Republican celebrity icon Sarah Palin.

"What's not to love?" I said, scrunching my shoulders as well. "You've got that right!" Miss Charlotte said. "I think she is terrific! I bet you're just like her!" she said with great motherly pride.

"Probably not really so much," I said, smiling warmly.

Palin, of course, has done a formidable job of turning herself into an impressive brand out of near obscurity while wielding money and support for other candidates. She seems to be most popular with those who think she is "one of them," and for the conservative faithful, she is a highly likable and charismatic person. For many others, she embodies what is so very wrong and simplistic about the Republican Party. How much of her persona is "built for consumption" and how much is real, I really don't know. Just because she can hunt seals or shoot moose doesn't make her the kind of leader the country needs right now.

"But she is very charismatic," I suggested.

"And I know you are too!" Miss Charlotte replied. I smiled.

After Miss C and I had taken a tour of the facilities, I retreated for a few moments of quiet into the ladies' room and went into a stall to look over my opening notes. After thirty seconds, I heard someone open the door from the hallway and holler, "Barbara? Barbara? Barbara? Are you in here?" The door to the stall jiggled in front of me as I saw the knit pants and sensible shoes below the door. "Yes," I replied.

"Time for you to go. Time for you to go onstage!" I sighed deeply and walked out. "Thank you, Miss Charlotte," I said to my beaming guide.

"Go be like Sarah!"

"I'll do my best." I smiled and took in a few deep breaths.

Although everyone had been pleasant, there was something in the air like a cool breeze before a storm—something that seemed a little reticent, as if I were perhaps the only Episcopalian at a Southern Baptist dinner. I put that feeling aside as I walked through the crowd of 250 mostly retired, but all white middle-class men and women to take my place at the podium. The only other candidates that night were the undertaker, Steve Southerland, and the pilot, David Scholl.

As we discussed the various issues—the Constitution, the immigration act in Arizona, the constitutional issues with the health-care bill—I drew on my knowledge as a lawyer, which, at every opportunity, seemed to anger my opponents. We always received questions about the Arizona immigration bill, and that night was no different. Southerland was the first to state his position. He stood in a blue blazer, blue shirt, and blue tie as he grabbed the microphone and began to speak as he walked.

"They threaded a needle, and they did so masterfully. They threaded the needle, and Arizona's law does not in any way infringe upon the federal government doing its job. It allows the federal government to do its job. So the question is, when does Congress, who passes a law giving them the authority in the Constitution, when can they totally disregard it? When can they ignore the Constitution? And I don't think anything in that Constitution forbids the individual citizens of the fifty states of this country from protecting their citizens, and I applaud Arizona and every other state that does the same thing."

I was taking notes, but this was nonsensical.

Scholl bounced up, happy as always. His teeth beamed as he smiled and looked eagerly around the room. With his shoulders back and head jutted forward, he said, "I totally support the bill in Arizona because of the Tenth Amendment. The law is exactly in compliance with the federal Law. It is short and simple and it is fine." He bobbed his head to help make his point.

He also mentioned his buddy, President Reagan, as he usually did no matter the question, though I forget how that worked its way into his answer. He said that he had seen the Arizona border "up close and personal" when he was in the Air Force, and finished with, "I have a friend in Niceville with a fence company, Niceville Fence Company, and if there is a 'Whataburger' every twenty miles, my friend tells me he could build the fence at twenty miles a day."

I'd heard the "Whataburger" line before. Scholl always laughs hard after delivering it while craning his neck back and forth across the room to be sure everybody else is enjoying it too.

"Oh," he said, "one more thing. We should have Arizona governor Brewer come be our governor in Florida 'cause she is more of a man than Charlie Crist is!" He punched the air with his fist while laughing. The crowd offered no additional laughter, and the room remained quiet. Pleased with his performance, Scholl took his seat.

I was quiet for a moment too, wondering how to respond to these bogus theatrics and the nonsense about the Constitution and what it states. As I stood up, I reached for the pocket Constitution I carried with my legal pad.

"I have not memorized the Constitution, but I have studied it as a lawyer for almost thirty years. Now, David just told you that he believes the Tenth Amendment gives Arizona the right to make laws regarding immigration. But that is not correct. Here is what the Tenth Amendment says":

The powers not delegated to the United States by the Constitution, nor prohibited by it to the states, are reserved to the states respectively, or to the people.

"Now, there is a problem in Arizona, and I support what Governor Brewer has had to do. But make no mistake about it; the right to control immigration is given to the federal government under Article I, Section 8 of the Constitution. It is a preemptive federal power. The purpose is for uniformity in the laws in the United States for immigration. We cannot have different states with different laws for immigration. We have had laws regarding immigration on the books since 1986. Those laws required that we control the border and have employer verification. We need to enforce those laws. But it is the job of Congress, not the states, to make the laws regarding immigration. I might not like it, and these gentlemen might not like it, but we did not write the Constitution."

I didn't know it then, but I had just made a huge mistake. I knew that questioning the intellectual ability of southern men is usually taken as an insult to their manhood. There are still some places in the world where you'd better be careful about downplaying a man's strength, smarts, or the size of his truck, and the South is one of those places. I compounded my mistake by staking out a position that education and intellect trump personal opinion and belief. As a southerner, a part of me knew I shouldn't have said what I did, but I was annoyed by their willingness to say anything, no matter how foolish or incorrect. "I have studied the law for thirty years, and neither of these men has a law degree. And that's just the truth."

Both men smirked at the moderator, who asked if they would like to rebut. Southerland nodded and went first. "I never had a degree in divinity. But that never prevented me, or my father, from teaching Sunday school. You do not have to have a law degree to read law. I have served for three governors, served on boards, and written laws that have been introduced at the state legislature. It's not rocket science. For my opponent to say it requires a law degree to solve the problems facing this country, that violates our Founding Fathers who said, 'We hold these truths to be self-evident'"—and here he gestured with his index finger and thumb pressed together like this was a point of vital interest—"self-evident, meaning that common sense, not legal sense, was needed. So I disagree vehemently with my opponent on that point."

I was thinking, "Teaching Sunday School is equivalent to practicing law? Can anyone believe the two are possibly related?" But as I looked into the audience, a number of people apparently thought this was a good analogy: quite a few heads were nodding affirmatively.

Scholl stood up with narrowed eyes, looking tense. "I want to thank Professor Olschner for pointing out I don't have a law degree." He drew his lips back into a tight smile that reminded me of a fox baring its teeth. It surprised me that Scholl would attack me for stating the obvious—surely he knew he did not have a law degree. I interrupted with, "It's Doctor, not Professor." The audience laughed.

Still clearly miffed, Scholl replied, "Whatever," and pulled himself up to his full height. "Look, I've read the Constitution. And it's no big deal. You don't have to have a *law degree* to read it." He looked at me and shook his head while laughing at how ridiculous a thought that was.

I jumped in quickly before the moderator cut me off: "The job of Congress is to pass laws, and I am saying that a knowledge of laws and the Constitution is an advantage when commenting on issues from a legal perspective, as both of you just did."

Scholl turned toward me. "The Constitution is no *big deal*. I just read it. I can read. We can all read," and he looked at me as if this should put me in my place. "I can't see anything so important about reading it for thirty years. It's just a manual. I read plenty of those when flying over the Atlantic."

I was trying to visualize a pilot reading a flight manual on a transatlantic flight. And as scary as that was, it was more frightening that a person would want to serve in Congress who did not understand the difference between a flight manual and the legal document that has shaped our country and been subjected to years of legal interpretation.

Southerland stood up. "I have another comment." The moderator nodded. "We don't need another lawyer in Congress. All of the problems we are facing in this country are because of lawyers." Scholl nodded in agreement.

I asked the moderator, "May I respond to that comment?"

"No."

Restating the rules of the debate, I said, "I think that would be rebuttal, since that is a new area."

"No—next question," the moderator said, and we moved on.

I did not see that the legal profession caused any of the current issues—the housing crisis, the two wars, and the economic disaster. Not to mention the devastation caused by Hurricane Katrina and the Deepwater Horizon oil spill. I did address this, but I had to wait until my closing remarks.

An older woman came up to me apologetically after the forum and said, "I am sorry, but we do mostly hold the lawyers responsible for what's wrong in this country."

And I said to her, "What exactly do you hold them responsible for?" She said, "I'm sorry, that's just what we think." And she patted my arm and walked away.

That night in Dowling Park, both men were so angry that they stormed away from the podium without shaking my hand. Neither cared in the least what the Constitution said about immigration or whether regulating it was solely a federal power. And neither did the people in the audience. They wanted Arizona to enforce and arrest and deport illegal immigrants because that was what they wanted. And the last thing they wanted was for anyone to tell them where the boundaries were on immigration, or on any other issue.

Bob Sikes, a blogger on the website Practical State, wrote:

Wow.

I wonder why Steve Scholl and Steve Southerland felt the need to go personal on Olschner. Eddie Hendry was not there. Usually the candidate in the lead gets such treatment in early debates. Both Scholl and Southerland are good candidates with good campaign operations. Olschner is a relative newcomer in the race. Is it that both see Olschner as a threat? Do they have polling data that reveals this?

Stay tuned. It's starting to get good.

I was surprised by Southerland's and Scholl's behavior. I had stated the obvious, which I thought was no secret. I never intended to indicate that a person had to have legal training to be qualified for service in Congress, but I also thought that it was fair to say they did not have a clear understanding of constitutional principles.

"And why exactly would this make them so angry?" I thought as I quietly wound down the two-lane highway back toward the interstate and the Hotel Duval. I wanted to talk with my campaign staff and especially my communications director. But I could not get a signal, so I tried to answer this question.

This country was founded as a constitutional republic, which means we are governed within the boundaries of our constitutional principles. We are not a democracy in the sense that the majority rules on any issue. The First Amendment, for example, states that we can "make no laws abridging the free expression of religion"—no majority vote can take away that freedom.

Thomas Jefferson was concerned about the concentration of power in the hands of a few, and so he favored a republic limited by a constitution. He pointed this problem out to the Virginia legislature: "All the powers of government, legislative, executive, judiciary, result to the legislative body. Concentrating these in the same hands is precisely the definition of despotic government. It will be no alleviation that these powers will be exercised by a plurality of hands, and not by a single one. 173 despots would surely be as oppressive as one."

A majority unlimited by a constitution is a "true democracy" but lacks any safeguards for individual rights or any minority. A constitutional republic, our current form of government, is majority limited, providing protection for individual rights. It is increasingly disconcerting that the party that cries "Protect the Constitution" is calling more for its personal preferences on issues, like immigration, than for upholding the authority of the document. Candidates and voters seem more interested in achieving the result they want than in whether there is constitutional authority for their position.

Does the conservative agenda on the right not want any boundaries that would prevent it from reaching its goals?

The stillness of that summer night made the angry tone of the debate reverberate more loudly as I drove along that lonely stretch of blacktop. I could not come up with an answer to my original question about what had made Scholl and Southerland so angry. Instead, I just kept generating more questions. And these questions were leading me away from my own party.

Did Southerland and Scholl accurately reflect the mood of the country by dismissing the Constitution if it got in the way of how they thought things should be? Could a male candidate with a law degree have gotten by with my statements without raising such a ruckus? Was the anti-intellectual, anti-educated, and anti-woman tenor of the evening the current culture of the Republican Party?

One question troubled me more than the rest: If the Republican Party, the party that prides itself on defending the Constitution and individual rights, promotes ideology over constitutional authority, are we dangerously close to losing our constitutional republic?

The rest of my drive back to the hotel was under a very black summer sky.

10

The Destin Debate

Seventeenth Amendment. Clause 1. (1913)

The Senate of the United States shall be composed of two Senators from each State, elected by the people thereof, for six years; and each Senator shall have one vote.

The candidate forums and debates took place every few weeks during the campaign—from the westernmost part of the district in Destin, Bluewater Bay, and Panama City, east to Tallahassee, north to Marianna, and southeast to Suwannee County. There were also a great many other events where the candidates could meet people and raise money. No matter how many people I met, there was always another person that someone thought I should talk to who might provide campaign support.

In addition to the meet-and-greet events, there were radio, television, and newsprint interviews. There were questionnaires, pledges, and position papers. There were follow-up letters and thank-you letters and invitation lists to events. There were hundreds of daily phone calls and campaign material and brochures and signs and mailers and advertisements. It took hours of thought and help and time and people and volunteers and vendors and logistics and design and wordsmithing and message-enhancing. But it took one thing more than any other: Money. Several of my supporters wanted me to meet Panama City attorney Martha "Sister" Blackmon-Milligan. In early June, we had lunch on the porch at Captain Andrews overlooking Saint Andrews Bay.

Sister grew up on a dairy farm in Eufaula, Alabama—the youngest of six and the only girl. She had been an assistant federal prosecutor, ran for state attorney (and lost), practiced domestic and criminal law, and was a prominent member of the horse circuit in her spare time.

Sister was at least 5 feet 9 inches tall, and that day she was dressed in green shirt and pants. Her brunette hair was curly and long and she had to flick it occasionally out of her eyes. She had the gait and mannerisms of the accomplished horsewoman that she was. I found her no-nonsense attitude very refreshing. When we met that day, Sister said, "You're a lot younger than I am." And I answered, "I don't know that that's true, Sister." It turned out we were both born the same year, and I was about six months older.

"What would have you do such a thing as run for Congress?"

"Well, it is a fight I cannot walk away from." Sister nodded as if that was an answer she could respect. She said that I was smart and personable and sparkled like a penny, which made me feel a little more like a speckled pup than a candidate for Congress. She gave me the names and phone numbers of her friends to contact for support, and her name and reputation opened many doors. When I thanked one police chief for taking my call, he said, "Hell, I have to. Sister finds out I didn't talk to you, she will kick my ass! You got any idea what that's like?" I said to him, "I don't but I do, if you get my drift." "You're a smart woman," he said, and we both laughed.

Sister is the type of character bred only in the South; she is her own person and makes no apology for it, not that I am suggesting she should. People told me they hoped I would not get on the wrong side of Sister, and I had no intention of getting on anyone's bad side. I both liked and respected her for the solid goodness and straightforwardness she projected.

"Without money, Barbara, aren't you just pissing in the wind?"

"Probably so, Sister, but I can't quit now." I thought moderate voters should have a choice, so I was staying in the race. But with money, a candidate could make any inane statement and be catapulted into office. Sister explained that she had already contributed to Steve Southerland, the undertaker. The Southerlands were a well-known family in Panama City, and many people I met told me that their prominence and business connections dictated either a contribution or a vote for Steve.

With the little money I'd raised to date ($45,000 to Southerland's $158,000), how could I reach the more thoughtful voters in the Republican Party who, as far as I could tell, were not attending the debates? The volunteers, concerned citizens, and my little staff tried Facebook and Twitter, kept updating my website, and worked as hard as they could.

My knee operation in April often had me on crutches with one flare-up or another. By the end of June, my campaign manager had to pull out. I had drivers to help me cover trips from one end of the district to the other, but at the end of the week, I limped back to Walton County.

The Friday night after my campaign manager bowed out, David Flannery, my progressive Yankee supporter, took me (or what was left of me) out to dinner at Café 30-A—a white-tablecloth, fresh-cut-flowers, and white-napkin experience, thank goodness. Flannery and I ate at a table in the bar, where it seemed quieter and there were fewer people to greet. I was so tired that neither mascara nor lipstick would stay applied. Over wine and cold glasses of beer, Flannery offered his help, which I needed on every level of my existence.

David, although a progressive Democrat, was also loyal, financially supportive, and smart as a whip. Together we had worked on a health-care proposal until it seemed like overkill. We were, after all, in a district where the Republicans' main issue seemed to be the exclusion of gays from anything: military, marriage, adoption—even the protections of the Fourteenth Amendment, which guaranteed citizenship and its benefits to all persons born or naturalized in the United States. Sitting there with his glasses perched on his nose, he surveyed my condition.

"You're exhausted. You look like crap. You need help. I can help. I know this stuff. I worked on some big campaigns for governor, senator, and president. I know how to do this. The only difference is that all those guys were Dems and rich. You are neither. But you're smart, as bright as any politician I have ever been around. And more than that, you have intellectual integrity, you're a good person, and you really want to make this contribution. Let me help you."

I attempted a smile. I knew I needed help—serious, serious help. Although a few had contributed with all they could in money, time, and effort, there were many more who had said they would but did not come through. Many people, even some friends, had applauded my gumption to go out on limbs, only to turn and walk away with the ladder. I was so tired I felt bleary-eyed; my face would not even make a normal smile.

Perhaps the odd smile prompted Flannery to say, "I'm not trying to get you into bed. I don't want you to think that."

"I don't think that, David. I don't think anyone is having sex this year, are they? Because as far as I can tell, that whole sex thing is on hold this year—what with all the national troubles, housing, economy, health care, oil spill—everyone is out of the mood. Am I wrong?"

"Yep, Boss, kinda you are. Sorry!" We laughed. The next day we started preparing for debates and interviews on the major issues. David was a brilliant writer and thinker. His views were way to the left of mine, but I was looking more for truth than for a certain ideology, and the information and arguments that David and I engaged in widened my thought process.

Early on in the campaign, some of the volunteers of the conservative mind-set took offense at David and his abrupt, progressive, and often condescending ways. They wanted to be reassured that David did not have too much influence. My own supporters seemed to be concerned that because I could tolerate another point of view on the issues, even a liberal or progressive one, I might be weak and easily influenced. I saw listening to others' ideas as the best way to learn the strengths and weaknesses of your position. A few days after my dinner with David, this issue was addressed at a volunteer breakfast meeting at Don Pedro's, the local Mexican restaurant in the Santa Rosa strip mall on Highway 98. As plates and silverware clanked on the tabletops around us, we finished with the weekly plan for volunteers, calls, attendance at forums, and sending e-mails and other campaign literature. At the end I brought up the topic of having "an enemy in our midst."

"I understand that there is some concern about David. All of you have helped in different ways, but I have needed someone like David. He and I don't agree on many issues, but the truth is, I'm more moderate in my views. In fact, until getting in this race, I just thought I *was* a conservative!" Given the wild and extreme views of the other candidates on every issue, we all laughed.

"We have problems to solve that are a great concern to all of us in this room—a national debt that is spiraling out of control, Medicare and Social Security entitlements that are unsustainable, the oil threatening our coastline and way of life, the serious job shortage, and the ongoing recession. We can't be stubborn or willful or just plain stupid when it comes to solving these problems. We must be open-minded and resourceful and willing to look at any possible solution. David and I are working to do this now, trying to get voters to see the wisdom of solving these problems, rather than just hammering home an agenda based on fear and a lack of knowledge about the issues. Now, one thing I have said from the beginning is that I will always tell you the truth on these issues, as I see it. We will not always agree—just as David and I don't always agree. This is how I am going to do this. I need you to trust that I'm giving you my best."

The next candidate debate took place in July at the Destin City Hall and was sponsored by the Okaloosa Republican Club. David and I had prepped for various speeches and debates, and we were both now getting comfortable with our roles. This was the first debate that David would actually attend.

The debate was held in the room where the city council holds their meetings. There was room for about 150 people on comfortable folding chairs. The dais was a semi-circle wood desk with extralarge cushioned chairs that probably appealed to the type of men who selected them. The candidates with constant camera entourage (Southerland, Scholl, and Hendry) had their cameras positioned toward them. The debate was also streamed live.

I had seen many of those in attendance at previous events—the campaign staffers, the volunteers, the family members. With so many already-committed voters in the room, I tried to determine how many votes were "in play" and estimated that maybe ten to twenty-five voters were actually undecided.

In previous debates, all the candidates answered the same questions. In this debate, the questions were taken from the audience and addressed only to certain candidates. Scholl was not there, but he sent one of his campaign workers to read his prepared statements. His spokesperson was a very nice and polite twenty-something fellow with short hair and dressed in Hagar slacks and an open shirt. Scholl's words, which we had all heard so many times on the campaign trail, sounded strange in another person's voice.

Flannery had slipped in at the back of the hall, missing the obligatory Pledge of Allegiance and prayer. As was his extroverted and personable way, he chatted with folks in the back of the room before finding a seat in the section to my left. This allowed me to look directly at David whenever the three candidates to my left were speaking.

A direct question that night to both Southerland and Scholl's surrogate was:

"Would you support returning the elections of U.S. senators to the states by state legislators? In other words, would you support the repeal of the Seventeenth Amendment?"

Dressed in a tan suit, blue shirt with French collar, and a burgundy-and-navy striped tie, Southerland leaned forward in his overstuffed chair to begin his answer. His shoulders rolled forward and, in a manner now very familiar, he closed his eyes for long intervals. His neck seemed to have disappeared beneath his shirt and jacket, which made me think of a turtle. But it was his answer that I found appalling.

"I am of the opinion that the men that met in, uh, [*eyes closed*] Independence Hall in Philadelphia in 1787 were, uh, pretty smart. The more I study them, the more I study Madison, Jefferson, and Hamilton, Hamilton and Jeffer—Madison were thirty-two and thirty-six years old respectively. What they did, the people they studied, the governments they studied, the, uh, [*eyes closed*] Greece, Rome, uh, Cicero, the, uh, the countries of Asia Minor, I am [*head nodding*] amazed at their wisdom. I believe that there was, uh, [*eyes closed*] also divine providence that also met, also met in that hall [*head nods*]. And I think what we have done is embarrassed their memory. And so, to that question, I'm, I'm [*head waggle*], I'm fine with that. The more we tinker, uh, with what those men did, uh, the farther we get away from their original intent, all men are created equal and endowed by their creator with certain inalienable rights and among those are life, liberty and the pursuit of happiness. And it bothers me that we have drifted so far."

And here, with some further theatrics, Southerland gave a knowing head nod with pursed lips to indicate disgust as he rolled his body back into the cushioned chair.

I was mesmerized by the complete non sequitur of Southerland's answer as he glibly found a way—based somehow on "life, liberty and the pursuit of happiness"—to repeal the citizens' right to elect their United States senators. Incredulous, I looked at Flannery, who had flopped his head on his chest in abject disbelief. The moderator permitted me to respond.

"What Steve has just said, Ladies and Gentlemen, is that he is 'fine' with taking away the right you have now, as a citizen, to elect your U.S. senators. Instead, he would allow the political machines in the state legislatures to decide who will represent us in Congress. He is 'fine' with the kind of machinations the former governor of Illinois used to appoint someone to fill Obama's vacated Senate seat. And when he talks about the original intent of the Founders, let us remember that as originally intended, the Constitution did not give women or people of color the right to vote. So, when Steve says we should not 'tinker' with the Constitution, he forgets that if we hadn't tinkered with it, neither women nor blacks would now have the right to vote." I turned to look at the only black person in the room.

"This is why it is important that we send people to Congress who actually understand the Constitution and not just give lip service to it. And by the way, Steve's quote—'all men are created equal, endowed by their Creator with certain inalienable rights, that among these are Life, Liberty and the Pursuit of Happiness'—that is from the Declaration of Independence, not the Constitution."

The audience applauded. I thought at the time that it would matter to the voters that a candidate for Congress would not know the difference between the Constitution and the Declaration of Independence. But one of the glaring problems with the current Republican Party is the support and encouragement for candidates and leaders who use belief systems and agendas—rather than objective knowledge—to make decisions.

Before the debate started, Eddie Hendry and I had chatted, as we usually did. "I just want you to know," Eddie said looking over his shoulder, "I've said I would support whoever wins this thing, but you are the only one I would truly support."

After the debate, Southerland's aunt, an attractive and energetic woman in her early seventies, came up to me with a wide smile and a warm handshake. "I just wanted to tell you, I'm Steve's aunt, and I am working for him, but I think you are terrific! If Steve doesn't win, then you can count on me to work full-time for you. I just love the way you talk!"

I spoke with a few others as I worked my way out into the lobby. I ran into candidate Ron McNeil's brother, John, who was wearing a red polo shirt. While John and I chatted, a tall woman with shoulder-length gray hair and glasses came up and shook my hand. "I'm Ron's older sister, and this is his other sister," and here she turned to point to a shorter woman standing behind her. "We have heard you speak a number of times, and of course, we're here supporting Ron." I thought I saw her eyebrows lift slightly. "But we both think you are wonderful! If Ron doesn't win, you have our vote."

As I turned to leave, I saw Flannery and Southerland with their heads together, laughing loudly. When I walked out the double glass doors to the parking lot, I heard someone calling, "Miss Barbara, Miss Barbara." I turned to see Southerland's elderly father—white-haired and heavy-set and suffering from what seemed to be arthritic knees and hips. He was sitting in a small waiting room, and his stomach was pushed out in front of him. His right hand was on his cane, and with his left hand he reached out to me. I extended my hand expecting a handshake, but instead, Southerland Senior held my hand and did not let go.

"I want this for my son, very badly, because, well, because he's my son." He choked up and I thought he might cry.

"Yes, sir," I said. "I completely understand that."

He let go of his cane with his right hand, reached across, and patted my right hand as he spoke. "But I wanted to say this to you, and I hope you understand." His voice was still husky.

"I'm sure I will, Mr. Southerland."

"If Steve doesn't win, I just want you to know that I would be very proud if you were my representative in Congress. I would be very proud for you to represent me."

"I thank you, Mr. Southerland. That is very kind and very gracious of you."

Everyone seemed sincere, and there was no real reason to not be. I had worked hard, I was well prepared, and I knew the issues and the law. But this didn't deliver the money, and without that, it did not matter how many folks had me as their second choice.

When I finally caught up with Flannery in the parking lot, I got another boost of confidence. He turned to me and said, "Why the hell are you in this with these morons? Are you f***ing crazy! This is unbelievably insane! You are way too smart to even have to be on the same stage with these nut jobs. Why *exactly* are you putting yourself through this?"

"Aw, thanks, David, you think I did a good job."

"A helluva good job, but it's wasted on these idiots. I'm sorry, but that's just the truth."

"What were you and Southerland laughing about?" I asked as David fumbled with his hearing aids.

"Southerland was sharing all his polling information with me."

"And why exactly would he do that?"

Flannery shrugged his shoulders. "He thinks I'm a writer from the *New York Times* following this race."

"What? How could that be?"

Flannery put his hands in his pockets and looked down like a schoolboy. "Well, Southerland asked what I did, and I said 'write,' which is what I *am* doing with all the crap you send me. And then he asked, 'Where are you from?' and I said, 'New York.'" Flannery raised his palms in defense. "Which is true. Then Southerland asked, 'And you are following this race?' And I said, 'Absolutely!' All of which is completely true."

"I don't quite get the leap from there to you as a writer for the *New York Times*."

"Well, Southerland said, 'I can't believe the *New York Times* is interested in this race,' and I said, 'Me neither!' And that's when we started laughing."

I shook my head and laughed.

"Well, I'm glad you were here tonight," I said.

"What good did it do? Coming to one of these events, and seeing this"—and here he floundered as he waved his hands wildly—"this is maddening." His sunglasses were still perched on top of his head even though it was pitch-black outside.

"I think I mentioned we were in the shallow end of the pool."

In his best New Jersey upset high-pitched voice—which I call screaming, but which he thinks is normal—he bellowed, "NO! No pool! No shallow end! This is the freaking KIDDIE POOL!" And he stomped off to his car, muttering to himself, "This is insane! It's crazy! This is impossible!"

It was all those things.

11

The Party Line

The weekend before the Woman's Club of Tallahassee debate, my mother asked me to travel to North Carolina to meet with a relative who was facing serious legal problems. I flew into Raleigh-Durham Airport, where I met one of my best girlfriends since college, Trish Taylor, who is also an attorney and has specialized in domestic law cases.

Fatigue followed me like a small cloud. It arose from a failure to orchestrate my schedule with the amount of exercise and peace needed to keep all the balls in the air. I fell into all the traps that many overscheduled people do: working too long, exercising too little, and eating poorly. All normal routines had been sacrificed to the pursuit of campaign success. Months after knee surgery, I still needed Advil to make it through the day and night. I was beginning to think that Dianne Berryhill, the Republican candidate who had jumped ship to become an Independent, had been right about the knee surgery being a really good reason to withdraw.

Early that Saturday morning of June 10, I found myself limping into a Raleigh Starbucks looking for oatmeal and a Venti coffee as Trish and I waited for my relative. It was the usual Saturday Starbucks scene. The swirling air of steamed and frothed milk punctuated the aroma of deep-brewed espresso. The music from different, but similar artists played lightly in the background. Ball caps worn in a variety of ways hid last night's hair.

To begin this meeting with my relative, I needed the coffee and lots of it. Because this was a domestic case, the court would rule only on such matters as alimony, child custody, child support, and equitable distribution of property. But because of the deep emotional issues involved, my relative had great difficulty being logical and sticking to the issues: He wanted an agreement that included odd and unreasonable demands that would give him what the law could not give: emotional solace.

After a long day, Trish and I finally drafted a settlement agreement he liked. We had a very late but cordial lunch, and as we were saying our good-byes, he expressed his appreciation for our time and advice. But before my plane landed in Florida, my relative withdrew his settlement agreement and raged at me for suggesting he settle. The more he thought of compromise, the more he saw it as a capitulation of his "principles." He didn't want a peaceful resolution; he wanted to *win*, and if winning required a prolonged and expensive legal fight, so be it. What I found difficult to understand, though, was the intensity of his anger at the suggestion of compromise.

I observed a similar mind-set on the campaign trail. Whenever someone, most frequently me, suggested compromise or moderation, anger blossomed into a black-and-white mind-set that tolerated no shades of gray. The premise was the same: compromise meant surrender, and moderation meant a lack of principles. On more than one occasion, I heard voters express with glee that rather than give in to a compromise, "they hoped the whole government would collapse." "Could they really think this?" I would ask myself. "Or is this just exaggerated talk?"

The Monday after my failed trip to North Carolina, I had to be in Tallahassee for three days. There was an informal candidate event on Monday night, an interview with the *Tallahassee Democrat* on Tuesday morning, and a debate Tuesday night. Flannery and I met for several hours before I left town to prepare for the debate and interview.

The *Tallahassee Democrat* editorial board had sent out e-mail notices to the Republican candidates for the Tuesday interviews. Flannery thought I might have a chance at the endorsement because as a liberal-leaning paper, the *Democrat* would probably not be impressed with the more conservative candidates. We prepared on issues that had been highlighted in its editorial columns, especially energy and the economy. When I arrived at the *Democrat*'s offices on Tuesday, I was the last candidate to appear. There were only four of us; Southerland was missing.

In my opening statement to the editorial board, I said:

"We need to stop pretending our issues are simple and can be addressed in thirty-second sound bites. These are complex problems for which there are no simple solutions.

"The economy is the most critical issue we face. We cannot afford for this to be a lost decade. We must jump-start the economy and reinvest in America in order to grow the jobs that we are so greatly missing. We must give incentives to small businesses to encourage hiring.

"I would suggest a payroll holiday on the employer portion of Social Security income to all private sector employers. This worked in the nonprofit sector and created eight thousand to eighteen thousand jobs. We need to consider giving businesses a 100 percent deduction in the first year on capital equipment. I would suspend the capital gains tax for twenty-four months to allow more trading in the housing and investment markets.

"But, more than any one thing, we must discuss and understand that we must deal with entitlements: Medicare and Social Security and Medicaid. They currently comprise 60 percent of our budget, and that is unsustainable. We must address reform in a fair and equitable way."

Flannery and I had prepared well. The journalists asked substantive questions and seemed a little bored with the other candidates' canned comments, which had worked so well in Republican venues. These were astute political journalists in a political town.

Afterward, I stayed and talked with editor Mary Ann Lindley, who is tall and thin with Annie Hall mannerisms. We shared a similar sense of humor and swapped political stories. Mary Ann and I discussed our mutual friend Charles Ranson (the Tallahassee attorney who had dropped out of the race and would give me his endorsement), the strange political climate, and the current anti-incumbent fever that had every political novice, no matter how unqualified, running for office. We laughed over the antics of the candidates who seemed to be competing for best American or best family rather than best qualifications—including the local candidate who said, "I want this job more than I want the love of my mother." That weekend, Mary Ann ran an editorial titled "Anti-Incumbent Fever":

. . . *Which is why I appreciated the theme of Barbara Olschner, a former professional tennis player turned trial lawyer from Santa Rosa Beach, a Republican "reluctantly" running for Congress.*

"I'm worried about how we talk in superficial sound bites, which allows us to elect people who are incapable of solving the most complex issues," she said. "I've fought fights in the courtroom my whole life and know you don't win fights by calling names."

After the interview, Eddie Hendry said he thought I had the best chance of receiving the endorsement: "They won't give it to me 'cause I ran last time and lost. Southerland didn't bother to show, so he's out. The *TD* is not about to endorse anyone as out there as Scholl or Ron McNeil. You're smart, reasonable, and more moderate. I think they'll endorse you." I hoped Eddie's read was correct, and it did seem plausible. I needed the endorsement to help me with Leon County voters. It might not be enough to win, but it would make a difference.

According to Southerland's Facebook page and the pictures posted there, he was campaigning that day with Marco Rubio, rising star in the Republican Party and candidate for the U.S. Senate, at a lunch event in Panama City. Two weeks later, the *TD* would give Southerland a private interview because Steve said he had been with his father who was having knee surgery. The private interview gave Southerland an unfair advantage because it allowed him to present himself as less of a right-wing conservative Tea Party candidate. The next Sunday the *TD* endorsed Southerland as the Republican candidate; it later endorsed incumbent Democrat Alan Boyd in the general election, which Steve won.

The Woman's Club debate that night at the Old Spanish–style clubhouse of Los Robles (co-sponsored by seventeen local Republican

Second Congressional District
Republican Primary Candidate
DEBATE

HENDRY

McNEIL

Thursday, July 15, 2010
7:00 P.M. to 8:30 P.M.
Woman's Club of Tallahassee
in Los Robles
Tallahassee, Florida

OLSCHNER

SOUTHERLAND

SCHOLL

Sponsors
Big Bend Republican Women—Capital City Republican Club—Dixie County Republican Executive Committee—Franklin County Republican Executive Committee—FSU College Republicans—Gadsden County Republican Executive Committee—Jefferson County Republican Executive Committee—Leon County Republican Executive Committee—Liberty County Republican Executive Committee—Southwood Republican Club—Tallahassee Republican Women's Club Federated—Tallahassee Young Republicans—Taylor County Republican Executive Committee—TCC College Republicans—Wakulla County Republican Executive Committee

Go to www.cd2debate.com for more information
or to become a Co-Sponsor of this event.

Flier from the Big Bend Debate in Tallahassee, Florida, on July 15, 2010. This is where the party line would be thrown down, and I would not be able to toe it.

clubs and committees) was preceded by a reception with punch, cookies, and pretzels. About an hour before the reception, a summer rainstorm moved in, and by the time of the reception, it was raining cats and dogs. This was the Tallahassee Republican crowd. All the local party officials were there, along with several elected Republican officials and local members of the James Madison Institute, a free-market think tank headquartered in Tallahassee that promotes an adherence to the Constitution, limited government, and personal responsibility. All the candidates' campaign teams were also there, mostly talking to each other. Despite all the free punch and cookies, it was not a crowd that wanted to mingle. They stuck close to their respective candidates.

One man was wearing white pants and shirt with an American flag tie. His hair was long and tangled and he smelled of incense. He tried to talk to me about some House bill that I was unaware of and became agitated over Congressman Ron Paul's libertarian views. I could not follow him or find a way to turn the conversation toward any relevant issues. Several of my campaign folks rescued me, and he went to sit in the front row. The serious and somber audience took their seats on folding chairs long before the candidates took the stage.

One of the local officials called the candidates to assemble behind the stage, where he announced that the usual random draw determining the order we walked on had been performed before we arrived. Eddie Hendry and I exchanged a glance, but neither said a word. Steve Southerland was first; I was second, then David Scholl, Ron McNeil, and Eddie last. As we waited to walk on the stage, Scholl tried to engage Southerland on the joys of RV travel, but Steve was preoccupied with brushing away white flecks on his navy jacket and did not respond. Eddie was more relaxed and at ease than I had ever seen him. Ron was studying index cards, which was surprising given how off-the-cuff he always was. An official told him "no notes," and with some disappointment, he put them away.

This was only the second time that I was uncomfortable prior to an event. The first had been two weeks earlier in Dowling Park when Scholl and Southerland had tag-teamed to say, basically, that

I was "too smart to go to Congress." I could not come up with any reason for my discomfort and thought that maybe I was just tired from travel over the past week. But also, the weight of what I was up against was mounting, and unlike during my competitive days on the tennis court or in the courtroom, no matter how hard I tried, I could not find a way to turn things to my advantage. It seemed to me the handwriting was on the wall about the ability to speak to the Republicans from a moderate and practical platform. Or maybe it was the atmosphere: The room was large and dark, and the heavy drapes prevented what little light was left after the rain from coming in the many windows. The crowd itself seemed somber.

As I stood on the stage between Scholl and Southerland that night, I could actually feel the coolness of the audience. I gave the first opening statement and received tentative applause. My volunteers reported the tweets and texts of the audience, which were not favorable. The audience was offended when I said, "The enormity of the challenges we face can't be solved with simple answers or thirty-second sound bites." One lady in the audience posted a lengthy review of the debate on Facebook. After detailed pros and cons about Scholl, McNeil, Southerland, and Hendry, she ended with:

> There was also some lady up there but I think it was a mistake. She disagreed with the other 4 candidates on many of the issues in which they were united as Conservative Republicans, and kept using the phrase "well, the answer is complex," as though we, the American people, were too dumb to understand what she would have to do when she got to Washington to make any changes. But it doesn't matter, because she won't be going. At least, not on a REPUBLICAN ticket. The other side might want her.

On immigration, I said: "We need to enforce the laws that we have had in this country since 1986. We need to control the border and have employer verification cards. We need to have less red tape for those wanting to work here and pay taxes. We need to deport felons who are here illegally. Of course we are a country where others want to live. Even with our problems, people run to America. As Republicans, we need more than the right policy. We need to have the right attitude."

The tweets and texts about me from the audience were: "Liberal"; "a RINO [Republican In Name Only]"; "Barbara BOXER"; "a Dem not a Repub"; and "How did she get in the Republican Party?"

And when I said, "America must be energy independent, but we must do it in a manner responsible to the environment and our natural resources," many texts and tweets replied, "Too liberal"; "Lib"; and "RINO."

But then came my moment of truth in the campaign. The moderator shuffled his cards. "The next question is one that must be answered with only a Yes or No. There will be no explanation allowed. Eddie, we will start with you. Would you consider a tax on oil companies to reduce the national debt?"

"No," Eddie answered quickly.

"No, I would not," said Ron McNeil. The audience giggled.

The moderator said, "Mr. Scholl?" David turned his head toward the center of the room with a bright smile as he said, "No."

My head was spinning. The floor I was standing on seemed unlevel. I started to get dizzy and wondered if I was either having a stroke or had fallen down the rabbit hole in *Alice in Wonderland*. I thought to myself, "I must not have heard the question correctly."

The moderator stared at me, his eyebrows furrowed. "Mrs. Olschner?" His question hung in the air, impatiently.

"The question was 'consider'—would I *consider* raising taxes on oil companies to reduce the national debt, correct?"

The moderator looked at me with irritation. "Yes, that is the question." It was clear to me that neither he nor the first three candidates had seen any problem with the question. As it turned out, neither would anyone else.

Of course, I was well aware that not raising taxes is the central principle of the Republican agenda. But what if it meant continuing to increase our sovereign debt? Wouldn't this be a good example of when we might consider raising taxes? I remembered Pfffen's demand: "Plant your feet. Do not move."

All of the other candidates had paraded up and down on various stages promising to make tough decisions for this and future generations about the national debt. They had talked with religious fervor about the immorality of burdening future generations with debt. They had waxed on at length about making hard decisions with their family budgets and scrimping on Christmas presents because "times were tough."

I knew Southerland would fall in line with the other three men. I knew the party line. And I knew as I stood there that night how my answer would affect this race. But I saw it differently. I knew that we would soon approach $14 trillion in national debt, and that amounts to 100 percent of our gross domestic product—a debt-to-GDP ratio that is unsustainable. If we continue to extend the Bush tax cuts, we will continue to increase the national debt. We must consider something, anything, everything to reduce this debt that threatens to bankrupt our country.

I could hear a small primordial voice in the deep recesses of my brain: "Don't go there. Don't do this. Who's to know if you lie? Go Along. Don't be stupid. You answer this truthfully and any hope you have is over."

There was also the matter of the Americans for Tax Reform's "Taxpayer Protection Pledge" that I had signed, promising that if elected I would not raise tax rates. I had been advised that it would be good for my campaign to sign this pledge, but I now realized that signing it had been a mistake. It was wrong for me to promise that, no matter the consequences and no matter what new information I learned, I would hold the party line. It meant that I would not exercise my full intellectual abilities in making decisions, and that would be a disservice to my constituents and blatantly dishonorable. I was ashamed of myself for taking such an oath—even though I agree with the Republican doctrine that less taxation is preferable and equates to more personal freedom. But less taxation under every circumstance is not always the best or the correct solution.

The revenue from all taxation is $2.57 trillion. Spending is $3.83 trillion. The deficit is $1.26 trillion per year. As David Stockman, the former economic advisor to President Reagan, once said, "It is simply unrealistic to say that raising revenue isn't part of the solution.

It's a measure of how far off the deep end Republicans have gone with this religious catechism about taxes."

I had not put myself through the toughest year of my life to end it as a coward and a liar.

"Yes," I said.

It was a hard landing.

12

The Finish Line

Nineteenth Amendment. Clause 1. (1920)

The right of citizens of the United States to vote shall
not be denied or abridged by the United States or by
any State on account of sex.

Tuesday night, August 17, 2010—less than seven days before
the primary election. David Flannery and I had driven up from
Santa Rosa to Tallahassee in Leon County, which had one of the
two large blocks of registered Republicans in the Second Congressional District. We stayed at the Hotel Duval, my home in Tallahassee.
It's a chic hotel three blocks from downtown Tallahassee on Monroe
Street and within walking distance of the Florida State Capitol. The
Duval's rooftop bar and ballroom overlooks downtown Tallahassee
and the outdoor tables and lounge seating attract a sophisticated
and professional clientele. There was a Starbucks café on the first
floor, and I would take meetings at one of the café's tables, meeting one person after another, drinking plenty of strong coffee. The
manager, Marc Bauer, and I had become friends as I stayed there a
night or two every week. He told me his parents took absentee bal-
lots so they could vote together and had cast their votes for me. The
young women in the café had been wonderful as I took meeting after
meeting during the day by the windows. The valets and bartenders
ran errands for me in what became my home away from home, and I

was so grateful for everyone's kindness. It was much needed when I was so often alone on the campaign trail.

Flannery and I were there that night for a function at the Capital City Medical Society and to prepare for my last radio interview before the election. We were meeting J. T. and Tonya Ehrhardt, the wonderful young couple who were my co-chairs for volunteers in Leon County. Attractive, smart, and kind, they are people of remarkable character. Tonya was a member of the 9–12 Project in Tallahassee when she contacted me to discuss my candidacy. (9–12 is a volunteer citizens' group; the numbers refer to nine principles and twelve values attributed to the Founding Fathers.) She resigned from 9–12 to serve with J. T. as my Leon County co-chairs for volunteers. They knew the conservative bent of the Tallahassee voters and had changed from "No Party Affiliation" to Republican in order to vote in the primary.

My first radio interview with Preston Scott of WFLA had been positive, and this was an opportunity to connect with Leon County voters once more before the election. But there were concerns. My stock was falling in conservative circles, if it had ever been high. Flannery wondered if there could possibly be enough thoughtful Republican voters in the Second District for me to have a chance. The fallout from the Woman's Club of Tallahassee debate had been damaging, and they didn't want me to say anything else that would sink my stock further.

We met in the Hotel Duval's Don Shula Restaurant, a small, intimate bar and restaurant nestled in the southeastern corner of the hotel. That night the four of us had a table off the bar in the center of the restaurant. J. T. and I had Blue Moon beers, Flannery had a martini, and Tonya, expecting their first child, drank iced tea. Flannery ordered appetizers for everyone and seemed to take command of the wait-staff in general. He had become a mountain of support. You hope and expect that friends will lend you a hand with their time and talents, but it is an unexpected grace to have a stranger so generous with such support.

Flannery was too smart, too talented, and too young to be retired. But for the demon of cancer, he would have been at the top of his game, swearing in a raucous New Jersey voice and making decisions affecting millions of dollars in the health-care industry while ordering around his staff of bright, eager young executive wanna-bes. Instead, he was working without staff—just him and his Mac and his high-powered mental abilities. Occasionally, he would comment on all the work we had to do without people to assist us, saying, "I used to have peeps, you know." And I would reply, "Didn't we all?"

Flannery and I were far from each other on the political spectrum, but we were united in solving problems with sound, reasonable ideas. And we both came from the private sector, where you are required to produce. And that was the way we worked together. We also both came from a place of intellectual honesty that requires being open to a true dialogue of ideas rather than hewing to preconceived ideology. That night, at the end of a brutal campaign, we were both dog-tired, but we knew what we had to do in Tallahassee.

In 2010, there were 150,000 registered Republican voters in the Second Congressional District—42,000 in Leon County and 48,000 in Bay County. The other 60,000 voters were spread out among fourteen other counties. We knew I had to pull significant voters from Leon County to have any chance in the primary. Although early voting had begun the prior Monday, this was my last chance, and we all thought the radio interview was critical.

"So what do we expect tomorrow?" Flannery started.

"Well, Barbara had a good rapport with Preston last time, so I expect that again," said Tonya.

"But a lot has happened since then," said J. T.

"True," said Tonya. "The Tallahassee debate, the 9–12 debate, the *Tallahassee Democrat* endorsement, the Tallahassee speech during the GOP bus tour after the BP oil spill, the endorsements for Southerland from Eric Cantor, Congressman Jeff Miller from District 1. . . ." J. T. nodded as Tonya trailed off.

David said, "What happened during the bus tour and the 9–12 debate? Anything?" Tonya, J. T., and I exchanged looks.

"Well, in my Tallahassee speech, I likened the BP oil spill and its devastating effects on the coast to our out-of-control national debt and the effect of that on our economy."

J. T. cut in, "Let's just say that by continuing to discuss an energy plan that is safe for our environment, Barbara has some voters calling her a liberal."

"Geez," exclaimed Flannery while emptying his glass.

"The 9–12 debate happened before you were on board, David. It was in June, and originally it was supposed to be a debate between only Southerland and me. But Southerland declined to participate."

"Smart on his part," said Flannery, swirling his ice cubes.

"So, it ended up being the Independent, Paul McKain, Eddie Hendry, and me. It was a fairly knowledgeable crowd, especially about the Constitution, and I had a good night except for two things."

"Showing up was your first problem and talking was your second?" David raised his eyebrows.

"One guy got very belligerent with me because I said I was not sure the Fair Tax was a sound idea at this time, and that to adopt it, we would first have to repeal the Sixteenth Amendment, which established the federal income tax."

"And he got angry because?"

"Well, he said I didn't know what I was talking about, I hadn't read the book on the Fair Tax, and that I should just ask Eddie, who knew all about it and supported it."

Tonya jumped in, "He and his wife were both wearing Fair Tax tee shirts."

"Eddie was sitting next to me at the debate, and he whispered to me afterward, 'You can't win unless you agree to support this; I learned that last time.' My second mishap was a young man who was angry when I said that the U.S. Immigration Bill of 1986 had addressed securing the border, employer-verification, and amnesty for 2 million illegal immigrants."

"Maybe it's just the way you say things," said Flannery, looking into his empty glass.

"It's possible. He was very angry with me for not saying a 'path to amnesty' rather than 'amnesty.'"

Tonya said, "Are you sure? I was standing right there and his accent was so heavy I couldn't tell why he was so angry."

"I think that's what he said, but when I asked him to stay and explain it further, he turned and left, saying, 'You just lost a vote.' So, other than those two things, it was a good night."

Flannery called out to the waiter while holding up his empty glass. J. T. and Tonya exchanged a glance. "The question is, what can we do, what should we do to get more votes? Is that possible? Is there anything that we can do?"

I was quiet for a number of reasons. One, I was really tired at the end of this brutal race. And two, these three people were so smart and so committed to my campaign and to its message that I could relax and let them discuss this, knowing they would hit every necessary point. When the bartender asked if I needed another Blue Moon, I said yes. I sipped and listened.

Tonya and J. T. were similar in demeanor—bright and articulate with a youthful calmness that suggested maturity. They would need it that night. J. T. leaned forward at the table giving his wife an adoring and complicit look. "Well, T and I are concerned as to whether Barbara can hold on to the conservative votes she has. We think if she isn't careful tomorrow, she'll lose them. The Tallahassee debate really hurt her"—J. T. looked at me with kindness—"Sorry."

I shook my head. "J. T., don't be. I said what I needed to say."

Five different kinds of appetizers appeared, and we all were grateful to leave the conversation while we sampled each one. Though no one wanted to admit it, there was a certain resignation so close to the finish line. Flannery was tired, in pain, or aggravated that night as he pulled the ripcord on self-restraint.

"This is about saying that she would consider raising taxes to pay off the national debt? Are you f***ing kidding me? What absolute buffoons without a f***ing brain cell between the whole group of them! Those goddamn f***ing idiots! What do they think will happen to this country economically if we don't raise taxes? Don't they realize this is the lowest tax rate in I don't know how many years? Maybe sixty years! And look at the deficit we have! This is so insane! So she has to turn into a f***ing moron like the rest of them to keep from having the holy crap beat outta her?"

Tonya waded into the maelstrom. "David, that's not what we're saying. We're merely pointing out what we're hearing here in Tallahassee, through our friends and contacts, the 9–12 group, the young Republicans. These are the folks that listen to Preston and who'll be listening tomorrow."

J. T. moved in to help his wife. "We just want Barbara to know what she is likely to expect and the way things are moving against her. Sorry."

Flannery went ballistic from his frustration and outrage at being in the wrong camp with the right person. "You both need a f***ing bigger view of the world," David screamed. "You are not viewing these problems from anything but a low-level perspective. You need to get some perspective from a higher view. You have not lived long enough or studied these issues enough to know what you're saying."

I cut him off. "David, David. That's enough of the f-bombs."

"That's just the way I talk, I don't mean anything by it—my children talk that way, my mother talks that way." Tonya and I laughed as Tonya rolled her eyes.

I replied quietly, "But I don't talk that way, David, and neither does Tonya. So please. Say whatever, but stop the f-bombs. I'm just asking you."

Tonya said, "Look, I don't care. I'm not trying to have a political discussion about the right view versus the wrong view. I'm just saying, if Barbara is not careful tomorrow with Preston, it could be . . . well, I just think, and J. T. thinks, she has to be really careful."

"How does she 'be careful' when telling the goddamn friggin' truth? Can I say 'goddamn'?" Flannery looked at me.

"I would rather you didn't," I said. "Is cussing necessary?"

"Something is," Flannery said as he looked for the waiter again. "She has spoken truthfully about every issue, and everyone knows it. She has offered a reasonable plan on immigration that does not include 'busing back the Mexicans.' She is against 'blowing up the mosque' because of that silly First Amendment freedom-of-religion thing. She does not think that gays in the military is much of an issue in the face of 9 million lost jobs, a failing housing market, and a collapsing financial system. And she needs to be Freaking Careful? To not lose votes? Why the hell should she even show up if she has to be careful? What would be the friggin' point?" Flannery was raging as he got up to go straight to the bar.

Tonya waited for Flannery to come back as she gave me a tired smile. "Look, David, we're not political advisors; we're volunteers, and we're not trying to give any real political advice. We love Barbara and what she stands for, and we know it is right for this country. We just know what the conversation is out there and what may happen tomorrow. That's all."

J. T. weighed in, "David, we don't want to debate with you about politics. This is about thinking that Barbara should be careful because it seems the conservatives are looking for anything to go after her. Sorry again." He smiled at me, and we clinked mugs.

"The thing I don't understand, the thing that still confuses me, is the amount of anger because I said I would *consider* raising taxes, not that I said I was *for* raising taxes and not that I said I would *vote* for raising taxes. I don't understand why the voters are mad that I would look at all options. Do y'all understand that?"

Tonya said, "Well, from the e-mail traffic, they feel like you are not one of them. You are not 'just like they are,' and you think something different than they think, and that makes you an enemy."

J. T. chimed in. "You needed to say no to abortion, no to gays in the military, no to gay adoption, no to gay marriage, no to taxes, no to global warming, and hell no to any compromise."

"Oh, that reminds me," I said as I picked up my Blackberry. "Look at this text I got from a voter: 'I voted for you, but I will be watching you on abortion and gay adoption.'"

Flannery gave me a hard look. "Did you reply?"

"Yeah. I said I was not planning on having an abortion and I would think about adopting a gay baby." Tonya and I laughed.

"You're kidding, right?" Flannery shook his head. "You know, sooner or later you are going to realize you're in the wrong party."

"Gosh, I hope not, David. I hope there's room in the tent for differing views."

What I remember more vividly than the actual dialogue that night was the emotion at the table. My young friends wanted me to not commit political hari-kari because they had come to both care about me and believe in the stand of this campaign. Flannery, who could see the issues clearly and the lack of realism in certain Republican views, was frustrated at a campaign based on truth in a race where if you spoke the truth, you got killed. By the time the desserts came, the emotion had diminished.

"First of all, I want to say I have enjoyed the verbal food fight and feel everyone has acquitted themselves in an exemplary manner. David, thank you for dropping the f-bombs, I mean, stopping the f-bombs." I smiled and Flannery shrugged, "I'm from New Jersey, what can I say?"

"I know what I'm going to do tomorrow," I said.

Flannery pushed apple pie around on his plate. "I need to say something first." I turned to look at him. "I think I'm wrong. Not about what I have said, because I know that I'm correct. But about what you need to do tomorrow. J. T. and Tonya are correct. You need to say whatever you need to say to get any votes you can get."

Tonya answered in her soft but firm manner, "Well, that is not what we said. Not 'whatever'—just that she might want to be mindful of the strong conservative audience that tunes into Preston's show."

Flannery looked down as he shrugged. "Look," he said, "the truth is you need to save yourself. It doesn't matter. It's over. You can't win." He had the serious but sad look of someone honor-bound to deliver bad news. "The only thing you can do is save yourself. Why subject yourself to another beating by speaking truthfully? It's not going to do any good. All you're going to do is get the hell beat out of you by these right-wing nuts who don't have the intellect to understand the issues or the difference between an honest, intelligent candidate and a bunch of goofy guys who don't have a clue about what the real issues are."

David pushed his reading glasses back on his head and rubbed his eyes with both hands. I knew how tired I was deep in my soul and could see David's exhaustion as well. He lifted his head to a quiet and somber table. "Save yourself. It's over. What would be the point of you taking another hit?"

I smiled, seeing how calm they all were. "Well, it may be corny, it may be the wrong thing to do politically, but I entered this race with a mission to be truthful, both about the state of this country and what's needed to solve these problems. I see no point at this late date in trying to save myself."

"No," Flannery interrupted me, as he reached out to touch my arm. "Maybe I've had too much to drink. Just say whatever you need to say to get whatever votes you can get."

"That's not the point."

"Well, what the hell would be?" David pushed back from the table. "The point of running is to win, and you have lost, and we all know it. *It is over*. Just take the Republican line and forget about it. Say you would extend the Bush tax cuts; forget about what that will do to increase our national debt. Repeat the 'drill, baby, drill' line on offshore drilling. Ruin our environment and jeopardize our economy. It's working for Sarah Palin as the Mama Grizzly. Blow up the mosque! Bus back the Mexicans! Say something really 'thought-provoking' like, 'We're not going to take it and we've had enough!'"

"No, David, I can finish the race I started. I can take whatever criticism comes. I am not interested in being a martyr. The point is to run the race that I think is important. Speaking the truth no matter the consequences—well, that seems to be my race."

Flannery looked evenly at me. "I have worked for some great people and fine politicians. You are, without question, the lousiest politician I have ever known. You are, also, the finest person I have ever worked for. You will, however, get killed in this election."

"We'll see. Maybe." I stood up from the table and looked at the tired, kind, and somewhat defeated faces of my friends. "It will be fine. I thank you so much. I know what I need to do and without this discussion tonight, I would not have known. I'm going to bed."

Everyone rose and we all walked into the lobby. J. T. and Tonya and I hugged, and J. T. and David shook hands. Tonya patted David on the arm as she said graciously, "David, you may be a Yankee, but you are our Yankee." David reached out and hugged her.

Flannery and I rode in the small elevator to the sixth floor, which at the Duval smells of lavender and rose. We were both quiet. Flannery had his canvas briefcase over his shoulder, his glasses still perched on his head, and I could see his Catholic guilt rising. I was more calm and certain than I had been in weeks. We discussed tomorrow morning's logistics as he walked me to my room.

He stopped me as I put the key card in the door. "Listen. Seriously. Maybe you should throw your support to Eddie Hendry tomorrow. You like him the most, and your votes could help him."

"What?" I said, outraged.

"Just forget what I said about the issues. I'm sorry, but you've lost. Try to do some good and help Eddie."

I turned around, my left knee pounding. I could not wait to put on my pajamas and get in bed. "David, you're an ass. But, you're right—and you're wrong. I'm sure I've lost and that what I say tomorrow will make no difference in the outcome of this election. But it might make a difference for the next person who comes along who wants to tell the truth and strengthen the country. I've made up my mind. I'm satisfied with my reasoning. Good night."

Flannery dropped his head. "OK, Boss. See you in the morning."

Fortified in the morning by several strong cups of coffee, I was ready for my interview on Preston Scott's *Morning Show*. It was a clear, crisp August morning before the heavy humidity descended later in the day. The station was only a few miles from the Duval. Flannery drove and I looked over my notes. I had not felt this good in months. My knee was not hurting and I had slept well. "David, do you know what today is?"

Flannery looked straight ahead as he said, "Yes, ninetieth anniversary of the women's right to vote."

"Yeah—interesting, isn't it? I like that my last campaign event is on the anniversary of women getting the right to vote." We were silent as we drove down Monroe Street toward the station. "You know, to put it into perspective, I look at my family. Neither my mother nor any of her sisters were born with the right to vote. Mother is the youngest at ninety-two, and Sister is the oldest at ninety-eight. In the scheme of things, it just wasn't that long ago. It makes me proud of the things we've fought for in this country, and it makes me proud of the campaign we've run."

At WFLA, we waited at the back-door entrance as edgy and bouncy Eric Eggers, producer of *The Morning Show*, let us in. Eric and I had enjoyed a playful banter the last time I was on the show. I had given him some advice on his backhand, but I was pretty sure he was not the type of guy to accept much coaching.

We went into the break room and waited a few minutes until Preston arrived. Eric then walked Preston and me to the sound booth and returned to the production room to stay with Flannery. Preston has a deep, resonant radio voice and something Rush Limbaugh–like in his appearance—he is a large, roundish man with closely cut hair, round eyes, and thin lips. Although he is strongly opinionated, he is neither arrogant nor unkind.

The moment I sat down and attached my microphone, I began to speak about the things that were on my mind—so much so that Preston said, "When we go on air, can we start just where we started?" "Absolutely," I said.

"Barbara Olschner, candidate for Congress, Florida District 2, is here this morning, and we've had Barbara here before, and it's good to have you today."

"Thank you, Preston. It's good to be here this morning."

"Barbara, we were talking when you came in and you said that you are more concerned now than when you filed. Can you explain what you meant?"

"When I filed I was concerned about the agenda on the left, and the direction that it was taking this country. But now I'm more concerned about the agenda on the right. The parties are pushing their agendas for their own political power, not for what is good for the country. I am in the race for one reason only—for the success of America, not for the success of the Republican Party."

"When you were on this show the last time, I was struck by the fact that you did not seem to care whether people liked what you were saying. It reminded me of when I interviewed Fred Thompson when he was running for president." Preston pushed around papers on his deck as he rolled his head up to look at me.

I smiled. "I think that's right, Preston. Everyone wants to be liked. But I know, as you do, that if I'm committed to speaking the truth, not everyone is going to like that. You don't really like the doctor when he gives you bad news, but his job is not to have you like him; it's to cure you. I am not running for office to be liked; I'm running because I am equipped for this job: to tell the American people the truth, whether it's popular or not, and to make decisions that will change the direction of this country."

Eric piped in from the back room, "Barbara, can you give us an example of speaking the truth when it is not popular? Have you done that on the campaign trail?"

"I have a great example. When I was in a debate at the Woman's

Club of Tallahassee, there was a question that we were told to answer with only a 'yes' or 'no.' That question was: "Would you consider raising taxes on oil companies to reduce the national debt?" And my answer was 'yes.' Yes, depending on the circumstances, I would consider it. Rather than continuing to go to China and borrow the difference in the money between our spending and what we bring in taxes, yes, that might be something we have to consider doing. Now, the other candidates—each of whom had said they would make hard decisions, and that we need to protect our children and future generations from this escalating debt—they all folded like a cheap suit of clothes on this question. The first time they were asked to make a hard decision, not one of them could do it. The reason is that they are not committed to restoring the financial stability of this country. They are committed to getting themselves elected and to the Republican Party being in power. I am not committed to either."

Preston said, "Well, I just think some things should be off the table as a matter of values and principles."

"Well, I think it has to do with how big a hole is in your ship and how fast it's taking on water. If we're headed to a credit deficit like Greece—which top economists in this country have told me we are—then we're going to have to be willing to take radical steps to solve these problems."

When we came back from the break, Preston said, "Barbara, this is your last chance to tell the voters in Leon County why they should vote for you."

"Preston, as I'm sure you and Eric know, today marks the anniversary of ninety years that women have had the right to vote." Preston gave me a blank, vapid look, and Eric was silent. "Preston, you may know this, but Democrat women outnumber Republican women three to one in Congress. Women are 50 percent of the voting population but are less than 20 percent of the representatives in Congress. A more fair representation of the voting population will reduce the polarization of the status quo."

"Barbara, don't you think there are more Democrat women in Congress than Republicans because Republican women are out working?" Preston looked at me with a straight face.

I laughed. "I don't think so, Preston. That doesn't make any sense to me. These women, in both parties, would not be there if they were not women of accomplishment. This country is locked in bickering and political posturing. It is a huge stumbling-block to accomplishment and issue resolution. There are four reasons to vote for me that differ from the other candidates: One, I am the only woman. Two, the only lawyer. Three, the only professional athlete. Four, the only person to start and run a business on her own. I know what it is like to solve complex problems for other people, and I am capable of doing that for the country.

"We need problem solvers, not the political network of good old boys and can-kickers who are out for themselves and the people who support them only. We need leaders who are interested in the success of America, not the success of one party or one specialized group of people. I am running in this race for one reason and one reason only: I want America to be successful and Americans to be successful and strong. If you just want the Republican Party to be successful, and that's all you're concerned with, then I'm not your candidate.

"I can tell you something else. I don't have the backing of the political machinery of the Republican Party, and that is fine with me. As a lawyer, the client is the one I look to—I strive to do everything in the client's best interest. As a representative, I will be looking at the citizens of Congressional District 2 as my clients; I will not be looking at the Republican Party as my client. That is a big difference."

Eric said, "Barbara, when you are talking about sacrifice in this country, can you give us an example of what you have in mind?"

"We have to reform the entitlements—Medicare and Social Security. That accounts for 60 percent of our budget, and we cannot get a handle on our economic problems until we deal with that. I'm not talking about removing those entitlements from people who need them, but for those of affluence, we need to look at having them opt out of Medicare and Social Security. And that would be a sacrifice."

Preston said, "But, Barbara, I think what you're talking about is more accountability than sacrifice."

"I agree with you. One of my friend's daughters said that the baby-boomers are the generation of entitlement. And, being of that generation, I have to say that really hit me, because I think she was right. I do think the right word is accountability. But when you start with being entitled, you may have to sacrifice just to get to the place of being accountable."

I finished and said my good-byes to Preston and Eric. Flannery and I did not wait to hear the call-in questions or comments. There was nothing that could be done at this time to fix anything. I walked without a limp for the first time in months as we left the studio. "You did good, Boss, really good."

I smiled at him. "Thanks, David, I feel GREAT! I said what I wanted to say, and I'm proud of the stand we've taken. I couldn't have gotten there without you."

We walked out to the car. Flannery kept nodding his head. "Really good, Boss, really good. I'm proud of you."

In the early-morning air, I thought I could feel fall in the air. There is always a time in the dead of summer when there is a stray bit of cool air, a vision of another season, a promise of an easier time.

I did not know when I began this race that I would have to choose between trying to win and telling the truth. I could not star in this political circus because I lacked the character traits that would allow me to say anything to win. As a result, I was going to lose, and I knew it. But where I had felt confused and uncertain, as if I did not know the boundaries of the game, I now had clarity, and in that, I felt a sense of victory.

Because I understood more now than when I began: The strong views of the Republican Party are more about culture than policy or politics, and this culture lends itself to electing candidates based more on an ideological litmus test than on who is the best and brightest. No one party has the correct view on any one issue. No one agenda is more correct than another. The truth is closer to the middle than to any extreme. Leaving the rule of law for personal preference will lead us toward anarchy.

Flannery and I went back to Walton County, and although I won my home county, I finished last in the primary. For me, it was more about making a contribution that I considered worthwhile than it was about winning. And isn't that really the true joy in any undertaking?

Official Results of Republican Primary, By County, August 24, 2010.

Florida Department of State
Division of Elections
August 24, 2010 Primary Election
Republican Primary

Official Results

United States Representative District 2

County	Eddie Hendry	Ron McNeil	Barbara F. Olschner	David Scholl	Steve Southerland
Bay	1,154	1,610	977	2,917	14,404
Calhoun	27	65	36	137	320
Dixie	77	54	106	124	397
Franklin	57	60	78	125	239
Gadsden	169	205	80	523	470
Gulf	74	132	70	186	805
Jackson	128	294	163	933	998
Jefferson	59	88	34	194	242
Lafayette	39	27	20	49	359
Leon	3,092	2,354	1,530	4,897	6,143
Liberty	24	17	13	40	83
Okaloosa	156	401	379	2,311	499
Suwannee	420	308	282	638	1,540
Taylor	254	67	58	216	524
Wakulla	315	326	161	439	656
Walton	119	439	978	754	590
Total	6,164	6,447	4,965	14,483	28,269
% Votes	10.2%	10.7%	8.2%	24.0%	46.9%

The official results by county for the Republican primary in 2010. The good news is that I won my home county; without that, my feelings might have been hurt. I had a few third-place finishes, but mostly I was last with 8.2 percent of the vote.

ELECTION TYPE:		PRIMARY		RUNOFF		GENERAL	
CANDIDATE NAME	PARTY	# OF VOTES	%	# OF VOTES	%	# OF VOTES	%

DISTRICT OF COLUMBIA — September 14th — November 2nd

	CANDIDATE NAME	PARTY	# OF VOTES	%	# OF VOTES	%
(I)	Norton, Eleanor Holmes	D	116,277	90.18%	117,990	88.94%
	Sloan, Douglass	D	11,857	9.20%		
	Scattered	W(D)	798	0.62%		
	Party Votes: D		128,932			
	Smith, Missy Reilly	R	1,919	87.23%	8,109	6.11%
	Scattered	W(R)	281	12.77%		
	Party Votes: R		2,200			
	Tingling-Clemmons, Rick	DCG	229	44.55%	4,413	3.33%
	Stracuzzi, Natale (Lino) Nicola	DCG	195	37.94%		
	Scattered	W(DCG)	90	17.51%		
	Party Votes: DCG		514			
	Scattered	W			1,359	1.02%
	Noble, Queen	SHE			785	0.59%
	Total Votes:		131,646		132,656	

FLORIDA — August 24th — November 2nd

DISTRICT 1

	CANDIDATE NAME	PARTY	# OF VOTES	%	# OF VOTES	%
(I)	Miller, Jeff	R	Unopposed		170,821	80.00%
	Cantrell, Joe	NPA			23,250	10.89%
	Krause, John	NPA			18,253	8.55%
	Bryan, Jim	W			1,202	0.56%
	District Votes:				213,526	

DISTRICT 2

	CANDIDATE NAME	PARTY	# OF VOTES	%	# OF VOTES	%
	Southerland, Steve	R	28,269	46.86%	136,371	53.60%
	Scholl, David	R	14,483	24.01%		
	McNeil, Ron	R	6,447	10.69%		
	Hendry, Eddie	R	6,164	10.22%		
	Olschner, Barbara F.	R	4,965	8.23%		
	Party Votes: R		60,328			
(I)	Boyd, Allen	D	42,415	51.45%	105,211	41.35%
	Lawson, Al	D	40,017	48.55%		
	Party Votes: D		82,432			
	McKain, Paul C.	NPA			7,135	2.80%
	Berryhill, Dianne	NPA			5,705	2.24%
	Netherwood, Ray	W			16	0.01%
	District Votes:		142,760		254,438	

DISTRICT 3

	CANDIDATE NAME	PARTY	# OF VOTES	%	# OF VOTES	%
(I)	Brown, Corinne	D	35,312	80.20%	94,744	63.04%
	Fortune, Scott	D	8,718	19.80%		
	Party Votes: D		44,030			
	Yost, Michael "Mike"	R	8,919	45.72%	50,932	33.89%
	Black, Dean	R	6,871	35.22%		
	Nwasike, Chris	R	3,718	19.06%		
	Party Votes: R		19,508			
	Martin-Back, Terry	NPA			4,625	3.08%
	District Votes:		63,538		150,301	

The official results for the general election in 2010. Southerland beat Boyd decisively. It was a bad year to be a moderate anything, Democrat or Republican.

Epilogue

It is simple to follow the easy and familiar path of personal
ambition and private gain. It is more comfortable to sit
content in the easy approval of friends and of neighbours than
to risk the friction and the controversy that comes with public
affairs. It is easier to fall in step with the slogans of others
than to march to the beat of the internal drummer—to make
and stand on judgements of your own. And it is far easier to
accept and to stand on the past, than to fight for the answers
of the future.

Daniel Webster

On August 5, 2011, Standard & Poor's took the unprecedented
step of downgrading the U.S. government's AAA sovereign
credit rating to an AA+ with a negative outlook for the first
time in history. In May 2012, 12.7 million people were unemployed,
and the unemployment rate stood at 8.7 percent. Three years after
the 2010 election, the economy remains our most significant problem
and, as some say, our greatest national-security threat. Our political
pushing and shoving has accomplished exactly what we would
expect from two gangs on the playground: nothing.

My real purpose in writing this book has been to try to understand
what I encountered during my 2010 congressional race and
to share that knowledge. I did not write it to whine about losing. I
have been a competitor, in one forum or another, for a half century.
In tennis, I lost more than I won. In the courtroom, I won more
than I lost, but a few of those losses were spectacular. Victory and

defeat have been, for me, different sides of the same coin. I chose a riskier game of tennis because it suited me. I chose a riskier practice of law for the same reason. When, at fifty, I closed my law practice, it was because I wanted adventure more than safety, well knowing the risks that entailed. I ran for Congress for the same reason.

Helen Keller said, "Life is either a grand adventure or nothing at all." She had every reason to sit on the sidelines of life, but she did not. Another great adventurer, Amelia Earhart, said, "Courage is the price life extracts for granting peace." Running for Congress was a great adventure, and I am at peace for doing what I felt called to do at the time. I met wonderful people, on both sides of the aisle, with great love and devotion for this country. For a brief moment, it was my great joy to work with them toward the success of this great country.

To be candid, I was reluctant to enter the race: I knew from the beginning that it would be difficult for me to win. Given my experience with today's GOP, however, I feel even more reluctant to identify myself as a Republican. Although my campaign experience ranged from uncomfortable to disgusting, once I had begun, I would not quit. The more wild, senseless rhetoric I saw masquerading as public discussion, the more urgent it seemed that the voters should hear reason. The more intolerance I witnessed, the more determined I became to be inclusive. The more rigidity and refusal to compromise I observed, the more moved I felt to offer moderation. In today's political climate, in which partisan interests so often trump an honest exploration of the greater good, such an attitude might be seen as naïve or quixotic. I believe, however, that we must have men and women willing to take action to pull America back from the cliff of intolerance and polarization.

I stuck my head in the political buzz saw that had the Tea Party on a wild rampage in the 2010 elections. No amount of money would have allowed me to package moderation as extremism, which was what voters wanted to hear. While losing a seat in Congress for two years has no importance, the silencing of the moderate voices that will speak for the majority of Americans who need a successful America is significant.

I thought that as a candidate I would be talking to the same men and women who served as jurors when I worked as a trial lawyer. I was right about that, but wrong in my expectation that citizens would demand logic and reason from their political candidates. Because we strive for fairness in our justice system, a juror who expresses bias or prejudice can be removed from a jury. In today's politics, however, candidates and parties cynically play on the fear that gives rise to bias and prejudice. They do this to retain power and control. The people on either extreme cannot be reasoned into a logical position. Jonathan Swift said it best: "You can't reason a man out of something he didn't reason himself into."

The majority of Americans, according to every poll, are in the center on most issues, and tend to be conservative fiscally and moderate to liberal on social issues. There is no authority in our Constitution to legislate religious beliefs; in fact, the opposite is true, despite the assertions of the Religious Right. The First Amendment promotes the free expression of religion while also stating that the government will not make any laws "establishing a religion." The inference is clear: You cannot have a country where one may freely express one's religion in the presence of a government-established religion. Even the New Testament indicates support for separation of church and state: when Jesus was asked whether Jews were required to pay taxes, he responded: "Whose head is on the coin?" Caesar's, he was told. "Then render to Caesar what is Caesar's and to God what is God's." Wise advice for all of us.

Although I am personally a social conservative in line with Christian doctrine, I can—and do—distinguish between my personal preference, my religious beliefs, and the responsibility of government. These three distinct areas do not always intersect, nor should they. Sometimes, by insisting on approaching a problem through a single door, we neglect other doors that might prove useful. The federal government is not the answer to every problem. State government, civic organizations, and faith-based establishments may offer viable alternatives to many of the problems we want addressed. But this requires that many of us get off the bench and into the game. Sometimes it seems as if Americans want government to relieve us of our personal, social, and moral accountability so we can stay on the sidelines and voice our complaints.

I confess to being a RINO, a Republican In Name Only. Rather than an insult, I accept the label as a badge of honor. I believe in political principles, but there is more to solving problems than espousing rigid dogma. I am not intolerant of other views, even those of the Far Right. I want everyone to have the freedom to express their beliefs and convictions without being subject to derogatory attack. I reject any party's demand for conformity on all issues, finding that counterproductive for effective problem resolution. Most of all, I think compromise and moderation are great tools with which to govern because their use not only suggests consideration for all but also represents the inclusiveness that has made this a great country.

Republicans should also acknowledge the problems in our own party and work to fix those rather than just attacking the Democrats. This would be in keeping with the biblical advice to "remove the beam from your own eye before trying to remove the splinter in your brother's eye"—a principle that could help politicians retain humility, develop credible leadership, and clarify their vision. We would become a stronger party if we fixed our own problems first. And maybe the GOP should bite the bullet and tell the truth: If it is a party that demands ideological conformity on all economic and social issues—"the small tent," if you will—then it should say so and allow everyone else to go elsewhere for party affiliation.

When Republicans claim to be a party of limited government but make exceptions for enlarging government when it suits our interests, we are hypocritical. It is disingenuous when we claim to be pro-life but fail to address the high rate of infant mortality in this country. (In polls in which lower numbers represent fewer infant deaths, the United States currently ranks thirty-ninth or forty-fifth in the world, depending on the poll.) As a country, we allow infants, mainly in low-income families, to die at an alarming rate because of a lack of prenatal care, yet as a party, Republicans want government to spend money on ultrasounds prior to abortion. In our zeal to fight abortion, we have turned a blind eye to the reality of the deaths of infants.

And if we, as a party, really want government to do less in caring for the poor and needy, then we need to do more in contributing our time and money to our civic and faith-based organizations. Let us increase our efforts in that regard so that the demand on our government will lessen. Let's stop the angry and frustrated railing against politics and politicians and take what action we can wherever it is needed.

The night before my last campaign event, I said that I wanted to take my stand to make it easier for the next person. I want to join the ranks of those Americans who have stood for what is fair and good to make it easier for those who came behind.

Rosa Parks was not the first black to refuse to give up her seat and move to the back of the bus. In 1955, she was only forty-two years old. She was not physically tired, she said, just "tired of giving in." She was arrested, handcuffed, and fined; she lost her job and had to leave Alabama to find work. But her refusal to "give in" was the final spark that ignited a civil rights movement that moved our country forward toward fairness and equality.

There were others before Mrs. Parks. Eleven years earlier, Irene Morgan refused to "move to the back of the bus" and successfully challenged interstate segregation in the 1944 case *Morgan v. Commonwealth of Virginia*. The famous baseball player Jackie Robinson refused to move and was court-martialed for insubordination, of which he was acquitted.

But the desegregation of public transportation actually started many years before, in 1865, in Washington, D.C., when Sojourner Truth, a former black slave turned evangelist, integrated the horse-car system. Having escaped slavery and become a preacher and an activist for women's right to vote, she fearlessly told conductors that she knew the law and she was not moving. She gave courage to other blacks to ride the horse cars and moved the country forward toward equality.

It is never the effort of one person that causes our ship to turn to true north; it takes a lot of people over a great deal of time, and at times the effort seems useless. Taking the right step for the right reason is always the correct response.

The abolition of slavery did not happen overnight: it took two hundred years. The right of black men to vote followed the end of the Civil War in 1868 with the passage of the Thirteenth Amendment, but it took seventy years for women to achieve the same right. For blacks to be afforded the same civil rights and liberties as whites took much longer, until the Civil Rights Act of 1964. And when President Johnson signed it, he said, assessing the political fallout of the act on his own career, "There goes the South." Risks and consequences always come with taking the right stand.

One of the wonderful things about this country has always been the wide and deep moral compass of its citizens, no matter the race, gender, or social class. We are, and have been, a good, kind, and wise people. I have every expectation that we will remain so.

The naïveté that allowed me to run for office, that compelled me to commit to speaking the truth, that made me put reason over politics and wisdom over winning is, quite frankly, a fiber in my DNA. But that fiber is not unique to me. The ability to overcome great obstacles and challenges forms part of the DNA of the American people and the character and soul of this country. That DNA has been passed on to us by our parents and grandparents, some of whom belong to what is called the Greatest Generation.

When Japan attacked Pearl Harbor on December 7, 1941, my mother was part of a combined choir assembled to sing Handel's *Messiah* at Memorial Coliseum in Raleigh, North Carolina. Air-raid sirens sounded in the skies over Raleigh, and everyone involved in the production left the Coliseum, rushed into the streets, and looked up at the sky and at each other until someone heard the news over the radio and delivered it to my mother and the other shocked young Americans around her. At that moment, the country's military ranked seventeenth in the world. Germany had 6.8 million men (136 divisions) trained and ready for war. The United States had a half million (five divisions). We were just coming out of the Great Depression. But three and a half years later, the United States launched the largest land, sea, and air operation in history at Normandy and went on to defeat both the Germans and the Japanese.

The Greatest Generation did their part, and did it magnificently. We are capable of accomplishing a similar success. But it will take compromise, moderation, respect, civility, and coming together for the greater good. I am optimistic because I believe that the greatness of America is in its people, not in its government. Like the

Greatest Generation, I believe that there is an inherent goodness, kindness, and compassion in the American people, and that we have the ability to solve our problems through compromise and moderation.

Research released by Pew on June 4, 2012, indicates that the values and basic beliefs of Americans are more polarized along partisan lines than at any point in the past twenty-five years. It says that Democrats are more liberal and Republicans are more conservative—hardly a surprise to those following the unfolding political drama. According to the data, there are more political independents in 2012 than at any point in the last seventy-five years. Thirty-eight percent are identified as Independents, 24 percent as Republicans, and 32 percent as Democrats.

The Moderate Majority has the power to step forward, and the purpose of this book is to encourage citizens to do so. If you self-identify as moderate or centrist, then I ask you to be willing, first and foremost, just to say so. When people use the political hand grenades of labels to discount the person with a message of moderation or compromise, we need to remember that such an attack arises not from reason but from fear of the message.

Some have said that my political experience is unique to the Florida Panhandle and is not representative of the national party. But all one has to do is look at the national presidential primary race to see the same attitudes displayed that I encountered in Congressional District 2. The most conservative candidates (Cain, Romney, Perry, Bachman, Santorum, and Gingrich) led the pack, with the moderate candidates (Huntsman and Johnson) trailing far behind with only 1 or 2 percent of the vote.

Governor Perry thought Texas seceding from the Union was a good thing and described Medicare and Social Security as unconstitutional. Gingrich talked about the national debt and deficit while, without a prayer of receiving the nomination, saddling the taxpayers with a bill for $40,000 a day for Secret Service protection. He calls Romney a "Massachusetts Moderate," which translates to those who can hear the dog whistle as a Yankee, first and foremost, who cannot be trusted to uphold our values. Cain was so arrogant as to either ignore or not be vetted on the opposition research that would have revealed the series of women ready to come forth and expose his proclivity for "social overreaching in the workplace." And Santorum, a member of the anti-intellectual club, called Obama "a snob" for thinking it was a good idea for our children to be educated.

Bachman, head of the Congressional Tea Party Congress, who looked like a trial balloon for a Palin for President run, pandered unashamedly to the right wing. She said she would most want to take to the White House, "the Constitution AND the Bill of Rights!" As every lawyer knows, "the Constitution" includes all twenty-seven amendments. This includes, of course, the first ten, known as "the Bill of Rights." So, what was she saying? She was going to take the original document, ratified in 1787 and the first ten amendments only? Notwithstanding that she can't do that legally—is she declaring that she would ignore the amendments since the Bill of Rights was ratified? That would include that blacks are no longer slaves (Thirteenth Amendment), and that they have the right to vote (Fifteenth Amendment); that all people have equal protection and due process (Fourteenth Amendment) and the right of income tax (Sixteenth Amendment); the right of the people rather than legislatures to elect U.S. senators (Seventeenth Amendment); and the right of women to vote (Nineteenth Amendment). (I could go on until the Twenty-Seventh Amendment, but I think my point is made.)

And lest you say I am an elitist on these issues, Mrs. Bachman herself is an attorney, with an LLM in taxation in addition to her juris doctorate degree. Clearly she knows better and is pandering to those who don't—or to the Tea Party, which is especially fond of the first ten amendments.

If Romney were to speak truthfully about the fact that he would probably govern as a moderate, he would be viciously attacked by those on the right, so he acts oddly out of step with the base—which he is. It is hard to vote for a president who is afraid of his base. I know what Woody Allen meant when he said, "These are the best minds the GOP can come up with?"

Meanwhile, a smart and accomplished Jon Huntsman, extremely successful during his tenure as a two-term governor of Utah, successful in business, and expert in foreign affairs as a foreign diplomat, not only dropped out early with only 1 percent of the vote, but had to spend time defending himself for working for the Obama administration as ambassador to China. He describes himself as a center-right conservative, but he acknowledges the existence of global warming, worked for our president, and supports civil unions for gay couples. He is another qualified person with the little-valued skill of working across party lines who does not pass the party's ideological litmus test.

I still believe in Republican principles, but not the hard-right movement that controls the Republican Party. I would like for the party with such a grand heritage to reflect progressive ideas like Teddy Roosevelt and show more commitment to civil rights like Abraham Lincoln. But for this to occur, there must be national reconciliation calling for moderation, tolerance, civility, and evidence-based decisions. We should refuse to be satisfied with superficial sound bites from candidates for office and demand more rational conversations on the issues. We should see using pejorative labels to destroy political candidates for what it is: an attempt to undermine the person instead of engaging with the ideas they propose. We will all have to get out of our comfort zone, whether it is by listening to and reading a wider base of media outlets, volunteering to feed the hungry, or perhaps, for a few, running for office.

And so a percentage of the profits of this book will go to a 501(c)(4) organization called "Purple Moderates." This nonpartisan organization will inform voters on the issues and on the candidates who promote moderation and compromise. We will also form a super-PAC called "Moderate-Majority PAC" to fund campaigns of moderate candidates, and we have a plan to unveil a list of moderate and centrist candidates. These links may be found at the websites www.thereluctantrepublican.net and www.purplemoderates.com.

I want to close with one last quote, from George Bernard Shaw. I have carried these powerful words with me for many years. Many times, during the 2010 congressional race, portions of this quote played in my head and in my heart, carrying me forward. And, yes, I am aware he was a socialist. But, to me, no hand-grenade label can discount the majesty of his words or their power to encourage:

*This is the true joy in life, being used for a purpose recognized by your-
self as a mighty one. Being a force of nature instead of a feverish, selfish
little clod of ailments and grievances complaining that the world will not
devote itself to making you happy. I am of the opinion that my life belongs
to the whole community and as I live it is my privilege—my privilege to
do for it whatever I can. I want to be thoroughly used up when I die, for
the harder I work the more I live. I rejoice in life for its own sake. Life is no
brief candle to me; it is a sort of splendid torch which I've got to hold up
for the moment and I want to make it burn as brightly as possible before
handing it on to future generations.*

Postscript: November 2012

Republican leaders were surprised by the outcome of the 2012 presidential election. They had not expected to win only one demographic:
white men over the age of 30.

In the postmortem, some said the GOP was too conservative, and
some said it was not nearly conservative enough. And although I am
an advocate for moderation, moderation alone is not the answer. The
GOP has a more fatal flaw: it lacks a national vision—a vision for the
nation as a whole, a vision that includes all of us.

The Republican Party has no grand ideas for the success of America, no great purposes to accomplish, no expansive plan for the nation. There are no bold leaders willing to point this party to higher
ground. Instead, the Republican vision for America is tethered to
a very narrow ideology, one that has resulted in a small tent with
limited seating.

The strategy for the 2012 election cycle seemed to be a recurring
negative theme that pitted citizens against one another. Voters were
challenged to choose between being "one of us" or "one of them." You
could only be a conservative or a liberal; a giver or a taker; a citizen or
an illegal; for or against gays, women, and reproductive rights; and
ultimately, either accountable for your own life or merely one of the
"47 percent."

Voters accepted the challenge; the "thems" had the numbers and
voted Democrat. They also sent their message: the era of a government run by paternalistic wealthy white men is over.

The GOP not only failed to see that such a constrained agenda would be so polarizing, but it also neglected to consider that it was asking to be trusted to govern an entire nation. And as such, it failed to demonstrate a sincere concern for what is important in the hearts and minds of all American citizens. Its purpose must be greater than the narrow banner of a political ideology that promotes only a minority of interests.

Grand ideas are always fueled by majestic purposes and supported by the virtues that make us proud to be Americans. High ideals that treasure freedom and democracy make us unique in the world. And no political party can expect to have the voters' trust to govern if those virtues are absent in its policies, its philosophies, and its politicians.

I have called myself a reluctant Republican because I, like many, do not find that the GOP exhibits the tolerance, compassion, fairness, and equality sorely needed in the creation of great ideas for America. I do not find that we, as a party, place the prosperity of America over the power of the party, and I find, to my great regret, that the success of the party, whatever the cost, takes precedence over the struggles of individual Americans.

I believe now what I believed when I began this journey: no single party has it right, and no one agenda has all the answers.

My fight for moderation in the GOP and in America is not that we should all have one identical mindset but that we must allow for an important integral ingredient that is missing in today's political dialogue: tolerance for the views of others. Intolerance is not a right enshrined in the Constitution and has never been the prerogative of any American.

The importance of moderation is that it acknowledges the value of disparate views to the wholeness of a grand society—the key, I believe, to the reemergence of the Grand Old Party.

Seaside, Florida, on the Gulf of Mexico. The beauty of this country is a reminder to us all of the need to contribute our time, efforts, and talents to keeping America great for generations to come.

Acknowledgments

I want to thank so many dear friends who gave so much of their time, their efforts, their encouragement, and their support to this book: Trish Taylor, Barbara Sue McGowan, Mary Marino, Susan and Lindsey Breeden, Freya and Bob Jones, Tonya and J. T. Ehrhardt, Lynn and Randy Pike, Ann and Bill Schultz, Jim Dixon, David Flannery, Julie Dorathy, Mike Oelrich, Howard K. Smith, Joe Swat, Mark Hart, David and Augusta Dowd, and especially the Modica family.

Eileen West was my creative maven through the awful and arduous journey of a major creative project by a neophyte.

David Minckler, my editor, was astute, smart and exceedingly kind as he coaxed me across the finish line.

Ronald Goldfarb, a fellow member of the bar and my literary agent, understood the importance of this message and helped to make this project a reality with his wisdom, advice, and encouragement.

Two people I admired very much passed away during the writing of this book: Charles Modica Sr. was eighty-eight years old, and my aunt, Thelma Lilley Blackmore, was ninety-eight. They were both the finest examples of those virtues we adore: goodness, kindness, and wisdom.

Barbara F. Olschner is a native of North Carolina who moved to Birmingham, Alabama, to create the Olschner & Hart law firm. After thirty years of practice, she moved permanently to Walton County, Florida, where she ran for the Second Congressional District and lost.